By William (

I WAS REBORN
IN THE FIRE

AS A PHOENIX IS REBORN THROUGH FIRE
BY THE POWER OF THE CREATOR

By William Cato Jenkins Jr.

I WAS REBORN IN THE FIRE

AS A PHOENIX IS REBORN THROUGH FIRE
BY THE POWER OF THE CREATOR

ISBN: 978-1-7947-0987-4

"The human spirit is resilient and wants to find its way home to wholeness."
One day I realized that I was happy, and soon after, I saw that I was thriving. I had been through the fire and emerged whole and clear, with doors opening in so many ways. The sad and frustrated stories in my mind had fallen away, and the emotions that had captured my soul softened. I can breathe freely once again.

ANGER

PAIN

HATRED

FEAR

SIN

DESIRED
FOR POWER

SUFFERING

I Was Reborn in the Fire is a story about my search for happiness through healing, self-care and self-love.

My name is William Jenkins, and I am the author of I WAS REBORN IN THE FIRE. I wrote this book because of a dream. Then I thought I was doing everything I could to live a vibrant, healthy life; but something was still off. It was in my discovery of self, my mind/body connection, and my opening to self-love and acceptance that I healed my body, and provided myself the foundation to live a life of optimal wellbeing.

The dreams of a phoenix rising from the flames of hell, rising from the ashes means to emerge from a catastrophe stronger, smarter and more powerful mind, body and soul. Sometimes you have to burn yourself to the ground (things will get worse before they can get better) before you can rise like a phoenix from the ashes.

A redeemed life is a transformed life. It is an issue of the heart, not primarily an issue of behavior. A persons' outward life is the result of what is happening within their heart. Any person can conform to a list of rules and regulations for a time, but if they are depending on their own ability to resist temptation, they will eventually fail.

Every demographic of people experiences hurt, pain and sin. All people relate. All live a life wanting to be cherished and loved, accepted and allowed to feel beautiful.

All want to be acknowledged and will go to great lengths to devote themselves to the one who acknowledges them, believes in them, protects them and desires nothing but what is best for them.

The moment we understand that we are all in this together, in spite of the various degrees of our experiences, we are taking the first step to not only self-awareness singularly, but self-awareness amidst the masses. No more should we feel we have to bear the weight of any burden alone. And since we are not alone, we can bring our self-awareness to the table of vulnerability and seek help through talking, writing, sharing our stories.

So as the fire burns, you will be rise up and leave your sins and ashes behind!

I WAS REBORN IN THE FIRE...

My hope is that, in reading this book, you will discover the importance of knowing and loving you.

In this book, I hope to inspire in you the same sort of awakening and excitement that I have for self-awareness. Ultimately, I want you to see this book as a tool to help you be present, embrace the perfection of you, let go of things you don't control, and live the life you deserve to live. In this book, you will learn about the connection between optimal wellbeing and root cause.

You will learn to know and love yourself, and follow your instinct. You have to understand your dreams and what is mean to dream of a Phoenix (color; dark, red, yellow, and blue). And the path they can and will show you.

Before you read, please keep in mind that I am sharing this story based on my personal relationship with the *The Creator*, my faith journey, and my belief system. You are absolutely entitled to your own opinions and beliefs, but please understand that this is not an appropriate forum for theological debate, this store is fiction and non-fiction it being done to help many to see the power that lies dormant within you and I waiting to be awake.

In this world, we learn about the nature of power, and the ongoing battle for our soul. We experience the difference between Satan's version of power, which is power over, as in power over others, and the creator version of power, which is power to, as in power to do good, power to love, power to create, and power to heal.

When we are feeling powerless because we are subject to the sins of others or the consequences of our own poor choices, what a blessing to be reminded of what powers we do have, what provisions the *The Creator* is making to reach out for us, and what good we can yet do amid all that we cannot do. the *The Creator* has been in all these hard places with us and for us, and knows how to guide and succor us in the loneliness of this dark realm we live in.

He has taken on the hard task of atoning for all our sins, and He desires all to receive this message of hope and salvation.

But we agreed to do something hard as well when we came to this dreary world. We agreed to come down here and get dirty, to face the indignity of making messes we cannot clean up. We must have understood that the goal of mortality is not to stay as clean as we possibly can, for if that were the goal our best course would be to never take on the incredible risks of trying to parent, to help, to discern, or to grow.

These tasks are simply so difficult that we will inevitably fail at them. No doctor lives up to the oath of doing no harm in the process of trying to learn to heal.

No bishop takes the responsibility of feeding the flock without doing damage to any of the sheep. No mother parents a child without injuring that child's soul a little before she is done.

If the goal were to make as few mistakes as possible and return to the *The Creator* as close as possible to the condition we left Him in then we would be better off to lay down on the ground on the day we are born and never get up. But our goal is not just to avoid imperfection and failure. Our goal is to learn to do good, and in that process, we will all do some harm as well.

I WAS REBORN IN THE FIRE...

Only the atonement of the *The Creator* can make the risks of mortality worth taking.

When I am about the risky business of learning to create, heal, and bless in my Father's footsteps, it is easy to get discouraged. How tempting, when I fail, to say,

"Why do I even try to discern God's voice, for I am forever getting it wrong, and at such a price?

Why have children when I am such a poor parent, and my children suffer so for my sins?

Why try to help others when I so often just end up hurting them instead?" Why?

Because our learning is more important than our failures. How gratefully I read *The Creator's* words, "Fear not to do good . Behold, I do not condemn you.... Look unto me in every thought; doubt not, fear not. Such words help me to see that God's faithfulness to me, a sinner, is stronger than the cords of death".

REFLECT:

My story starts back when I was just born!

I was born on February 18, and on June 12th a few months later, I was baptized in the church I grew up in. My parents dressed me up in a little white christening gown and hosted our family and friends for brunch afterwards.

I'm sure it was a lovely day,

But I don't remember a moment of it!

The perks of being the eldest child...my baby book is completely filled out! Thanks mother...

I know we all are born into in sin, the Bible teaches that we are all born sinners with sinful, selfish natures. Unless we are born again by the Spirit of *The Creator*, we will never see the kingdom of *The Creator* (John 3:3).

Humanity is totally depraved; that is, all of us have a sinful nature that affects every part of us (Isaiah 53:6; Romans 7:14).

The question is, where did that sinful nature come from?

Were we born sinners, or did we simply choose to become sinners sometime after birth?

We are born with a sinful nature, and we inherited it from Adam. "Sin entered the world through one man, and death through sin, and in this way death came to all people" (Romans 5:12). Every one of us was affected by Adam's sin; there are no exceptions. "One trespass resulted in condemnation for all people" (verse 18). We are all sinners, and we all share the same condemnation, because we are all children of Adam.

Scripture indicates that even children have a sin nature, which argues for the fact that we are born sinners. "Folly is bound up in the heart of a child" (Proverbs 22:15).

David says, "Surely I was sinful at birth, sinful from the time my mother conceived me" (Psalm 51:5). "Even from birth the wicked go astray from the womb they are wayward, spreading lies" (Psalm 58:3).

Before we were saved, "we were by nature deserving of wrath" (Ephesians 2:3). Note that we deserved *The Creator* wrath not only because of our actions but because of our nature.

That nature is what we inherited from Adam.

We are born sinners, and for that reason we are unable to do good in order to please *The Creator* in our natural state, or the flesh: "Those who are in the realm of the flesh cannot please *The Creator*" (Romans 8:8). We were dead in our sins before Our lord raised us to spiritual life (Ephesians 2:1).

We lack any inherent spiritual good.

No one has to teach a child to lie; rather, we must go to great lengths to impress upon children the value of telling the truth.

Toddlers are naturally selfish, with their innate, although faulty, understanding that everything is "mine." Sinful behavior comes naturally for the little ones because they are born sinners

Because we are born sinners, we must experience a second,

I WAS REBORN IN THE FIRE...

spiritual birth. We are born once into Adam's family and are sinners by nature. When we are born again, we are born into *The Creator's* family and are given the nature of *The Creator*.

We praise the Lord that "to all who did receive him, to those who believed in his name, he gave the right to become children of *The Creator* —children born not of natural descent . . . but born of *The Creator*" (John 1:12–13).

But I feel that once most live some what, so you should be in your teeth years so you true understand. There are a lot of kids who are good for the most and some of should do bad things.

But there are some of you who would swear they was the devil child. So, for me life was good and when I gave my life to my creator it gets better!!

My life has always been bless,

Grace has all ways been on my life.

All people sin. Not just in the past, but in the present as well.

The lone exception is the *The Creator* who never has and never will sin. He is the lone exception because He is only man who is *The Creator* incarnate.

He was born of a virgin and He thus did not inherit a sinful nature. The sin nature is passed through one's biological earthly father, which the *The Creator* did not have. Most people blithely move on to the next phrase and assume it is simply making the same point again in different words. That, however, is not the case.

Growing up, we attended church on Sunday mornings and said a short prayer before we ate dinner. I always knew that *The Creator* was real, but I knew that He was real in the same way that I knew the planets were real or a faraway country was real–I'd been told about those things, but had never seen or encountered them for myself. (*Not a strong analogy, but I hope it helps demonstrate my state of mind nonetheless.*)

Then, when I went to camp the summer after 6th grade, I truly encountered the Lord for the first time. I experienced the close intimacy of the Holy Spirit and actually understood, for the first time, what it meant to accept Our lord into my heart. This was the summer I "got saved," which is what Believers often call the moment they become a follower.

Returning home from camp, I was never the same.

My faith was a winding path through middle school and into high school, but I never walked away from it. I found comfort, peace, meaning, and joy in the Lord that the world could not compete with. Late high school were years of deep trial for me.

My faith was truly tested for the first time as a series of horrible events, one after the other, sent me into an incredibly dark and depressed state.

The Creator was faithful to me through those hard months in a way that made me trust Him deeply and fully. I wish we could sit down over a cup of coffee (or tea!) so I could tell you how He redeemed that dark season and turned it into something beautiful. I could cry now thinking about it, and it was over a decade ago!

Fast-forward to college, when, for the first time ever, I had a Believer community through Inter Varsity *(an organization for believers on college campuses)*. My college years were mostly sweet, with a handful of spiritually-challenging parts that *The Creator* led me through.

By the time I graduated from college, I had learned through experience that I could trust Creator's plan for my life completely. Because of this, I applied to jobs all over the US, from GA, FL and to Texas. I was convinced that the *The Creator* would put me exactly where He wanted me, and He did!

As you know, I ended up in Atlanta GA, where about 700 awesome things happened over the years I lived there, many of which I've talked about.

Sometimes we feel all strong, like warriors, but then we feel like helpless creatures on this vast planet the next day. If only we had a magic word to get us through this thing we call life!

12   *I WAS REBORN IN THE FIRE...*

But as they say, to have a good life, you need to cherish both the happy and the sad moments.

Unless *The Creator* gives me a clear indication to go another way I will walk the way to the Holy Spirit. I feel a great yearning in my own heart to know more of the Spirit's power for holiness and power for witness. I feel a tremendous need to learn to rely more fully on his guidance as the Spirit of wisdom and truth. The life-giving, renewing my life with the fire of the holy spirit.

The fire burn where it wills, and you feel the heat and hear the sound of it, but you do not know whence it comes or whither it goes; so, it is with everyone who is born of the Spirit. Draw near to *The Creator* and he will draw near to you.

We will see the paradox in that statement today, because we can't even begin to draw near to *The Creator* without the Spirit's help. Which means that in our very effort to draw near to him, he has already drawn near to us. But that does not negate the promise at all: it remains true that if we draw near to *The Creation*, he will draw near to us!

We all are born of this earth through the fresh of mankind and we may walk and live our live. But some are reborn through the *(baptized)* water, our lives will start again with a new start, but other are still live there lives some are good or not so much.

But these who have been reborn through the *(baptized)* water which is by baptized have gave their life to the created because they saw their life would be better. But there are a some from where they sit live never has change for what ever reason.

But I would add many of else will be reborn through fire, all will not make it to this point some will never understand what is going on when this journey started.

Everybody is familiar with the idea of Phoenix symbolism – a bird that rises from the aftermath of fire from its ashes.

It symbolizes rebirth and eternity and is also representative of hope.

When you share your life's goals with others you make yourself accountable but, more importantly, you enlist those people in your adventure since they become your biggest fans and want you to succeed. Think big and share bigger!

So that's it. It sounds simple and we all know it's not. It's a lot of hard work. I also read a lot of books, watched inspiring movies, had a personal coach and did a lot of self assessment work.

(A Phoenix rises from the ashes of its dead predecessor. This is symbolic of rebirth, hope, renewal, progress, end of oppression, and eternity. It is no wonder that the beautiful bird has inspired many tales, poems, and even legends.)

During my time on the south side of Atlanta, one of my mentors asked me if I was baptized. I told him I'd been baptized as an infant, but had been thinking about young adult baptism too. I told her that as I had grown in my faith and read scripture, I felt the desire to choose baptism for myself as an outward display of an inner decision since I clearly hadn't chosen to be baptized at five months old. He encouraged me to pray about it!

About a year and a half later, I was engaged to Judy, and my church was planning for baptisms. I knew I was ready to take this step and get baptized as an adult!

Judy and I were living four hours apart at the time, so I called him to see if he was available to be there on the Sunday when baptisms were planned.

She wasn't, but I decided to go ahead with it and told my friends in on the east side my plans. We were all so excited!

Then, when the day of my baptism arrived, one of my best friends and co-worker, Rod *(who ended up officiating our wedding!)* pulled me aside.

He asked if Judy was coming to my baptism, and I told him that she wasn't because she couldn't make it to Atlanta for the weekend. Roy, and Keith said, "Judy is about to be your wife. I really

I WAS REBORN IN THE FIRE...

think she should be here for this. I think you'll regret her absence in the long-run.

Why don't you wait until she's available?"

To be honest, I was slightly annoyed!

But Keith was like a brother to me, and I respected his opinion. I thought about it and decided he was right–I really did want Judy to be a part of such a special moment in my faith journey.

Years after becoming a Believer,

I finally got baptized on Sunday morning!

NOTICE:

I had intended on getting baptized shortly after getting married, but finding a church community was much more challenging than I anticipated, as many of you know. After finding our current church, I told our pastor and his wife that I wanted to get baptized and was more than ready! They were supportive and excited and set a date–this past Sunday, July 28th.

Between the time when we decided on the date and the actual date, a father and his son encountered Our lord for the first time at our church and began their own faith journeys. The three of us got baptized together on Sunday.

THOUGHTS:

This experience was holy and sacred.

Having walked with Our lord for so many years, it was powerful and emotional to share a brief testimony of my faith with our church before Judy baptized me.

I could've spoken for hours of *The Creator's* goodness, faithfulness, steadfast nature, patience, and love. His fingerprints are all over my life!

It was a joy to share just a few ways I've seen Him work in my life and to share how He has redeemed and restored me throughout the past decade and a half.

Stop focusing on your past sins. Straighten out things in your life and focus yourself on the goal.

"Not that I have already obtained it or have already become perfect, but I press on so that I may lay hold of that for which also I was laid hold of by our lord.

Brethren, I do not regard myself as having laid hold of it yet; but one thing I do: forgetting what lies behind and reaching forward to what lies ahead, I press on toward the goal for the prize of the upward call of *The Creator* in Our lord" (Philippians 3:12-14).

People often ask me, "how long have you been saved?"

I always thought the day I was baptized was the day I was saved and born again. I thought baptism would do its own work in my life and the gift of the Holy Spirit would allow me to sit back and enjoy the ride.

REFLECT:

I thought after baptism I would have a supernatural shield of protection around me, blocking all sin from ever entering my life again. After all, I did agree to leave the old life behind and die to old sinful ways.

I anticipated this new life to be easy, never realizing it was actually the beginning of a battle to walk faithfully with the Lord.

My new walk met to me with immediate attacks from the enemy. Sin brought me down again and again leaving me to question whether I had really been saved.

It wasn't until a few years after my baptism that one of my dear friends and mentors taught me that Our lord followers are in a spiritual battle every single day.

You see, the enemy doesn't have to fight for you when you are already walking with him. But as soon as the enemy knows you have been washed by the blood of Our lord, he rallies his army and begins to fight against your salvation.

Our lord was tempted by Satan after His baptism as well and He used the weapons *The Creator* gave Him to fight.

16   *I WAS REBORN IN THE FIRE...*

He used the word, which is sharper than a double-edged sword. He obeyed the Spirit as He led and He continually professed His love for *The Creator.*

I believe my moment of salvation was when the Father made His Word clear to me, the Son overwhelmed me with His unconditional love, and the Holy Spirit led me to obedience.

It was when these three elements and my personal relationship with Our lord made a permanent home in my heart that I was truly saved and armed for battle.

NOTICE:

If you have recently been baptized or are new to your walk with Our lord, know it's not going to be easy and there will be times you want to give up.

I encourage you to have faith, believing the Lord has equipped you with everything you need to fight the battle. Read His Word and spend time with Him daily.

You will soon discover;

The rewards are far greater than the fight.

For the word of *The Creator* is alive and powerful. It is sharper than the sharpest two-edged sword, cutting between soul and spirit, between joint and marrow. It exposes our innermost thoughts and desires. Hebrews 4:12 NLT

When I think of all this, I fall to my knees and pray to the Father, the Creator of everything in heaven and on earth. I pray that from his glorious, unlimited resources he will empower you with inner strength through his Spirit.

Then Our lord will make his home in your hearts as you trust in him. Your roots will grow down into the *The Creator's* love and keep you strong. And may you have the power to understand, as all *The Creator's* people should, how wide, how long, how high, and how deep his love is.

May you experience the love of Our lord, though it is too

great to understand fully. Then you will be made complete with all the fullness of life and power that comes from *The Creator*.

You've probably heard it a lot and even said it to yourself: "This too shall pass."

But do you believe it?

Maybe sometimes, but on some of the down days, it seems like a bunch of words people toss around just to make you feel better. Everything has more they one side to it there is happiness and sadness, ease and pain, and much more.

The phoenix fire is a symbol of when mankind is going through the fire of life for the 3rd time. It when you have lost your way after you have given yourself to *The Creator* and going thought the water. In your path of life you will find many dark days and nights but the phoenix fire will burn your past life and sins to ashes so you can be reborn with the rising of the phoenix with in the flames.

Going through all of these while maintaining balance is critical. After all, these things make you strong. The one thing you have control over is how you deal with all things in your journey and how much energy you have to make the best of a difficult situation.

When we read this revelation in Genesis we read about such events as *The Creator*, Noah's Flood, and the Tower of Babel.

These are events which have made the earth's geology, geography, biology, etc., What they are today.

We must therefore also realize that what happened in the past is thus the key to what we see in the present. In other words, the entrance of sin into the world explains why we have death, and why we have mistakes occurring in our genes. The global devastation caused by flood must therefore have a part in any explanation of the fossil record.

The events at the Tower of Babel must be a considerable factor in our coming to an understanding of the origin of the different nations and cultures around the world.

18   *I WAS REBORN IN THE FIRE...*

Today, evolutionists deny that the Biblical record can be taken seriously. They put their faith in their belief that 'all things continue as they have done from the beginning. . .'. The prophecy in 2 Peter 3 is being fulfilled before our very eyes.

We feel we never will feel as it is going the right way, and everyone around us lives are still moving forward. To rise like a phoenix from the ashes means to emerge from a catastrophe stronger, smarter and more powerful.

An example of rising like a phoenix from the ashes is someone who opens a new, successful business after his previous business has failed.

REFLECT RESEARCH:

The phoenix bird is a mythical bird from Greek mythology.

In the worst of times, it teaches us how to be victorious. Out of suffering, we grow in spirit. In heartbreak and sadness, this beautiful and gentle creature sings an enchanting song that summons the forces of heaven.

Relax and calm your mind as you observe the red candle's flame. See the flame alive within the core of your being. Focus on this inner flame's optimism, renewal, rebirth, and hope. End your meditation by thanking the phoenix for its guidance.

I believe as we go through much of our pain, we are being tutored, as *The Creator* was, in the sacred work of learning to succor one another. Much of our learning in (and gaining wisdom in) mortality comes from our pain and the developmental growth that happens as we work through each lesson.

Passing that wisdom to others along our path — whether by our compassionate, non-judgmental presence in the lives of others or by our willingness to share what we have learned that may be helpful to lift their pain — is our commission.

It is the most vulnerable and humbling experience I know.

It is understood that all we can do is drop the rope ladder into the abyss of another's pain. You cannot climb it for them. You can't heal the people you love, nor make choices for them.

You can't rescue them. However, you can promise they won't journey alone, and loan them your map. You can shine a light into their darkness, but you cannot tell them what to see. The trip is theirs. Be gentle with yourself. It's hard work to be present to the freedom of the other.

NOTICE:

As I am nearing my birthday, although in great health, I am acutely aware that I am standing in the closing season of my moral existence and reviewing what I have done with the "dash" in my life. I wonder if I've learned what I need to know and done what I was supposed to do. Is there more to learn before I return home?

The Phoenix is a mythical sacred fire-bird that can be found in many mythologies from the ancient Greeks, Egyptians and Romans. The legend of the Phoenix has been around for centuries, it's a supernatural creature with a life of a thousand years.

Once its life is up it will cast itself in flames, and as it dies it will be reborn again from its own ashes. The Phoenix has long been presented as a symbol of rebirth, immortality, and renewal. The Phoenix can be interpreted in various ways; lets explore and define this mythical creature that is reborn from its ashes.

What does the Phoenix tell us, we will first explore in my view and representation of the Phoenix? We can concentrate on the flaming burning death of the bird.

"The rotten fabric of our repose connives with doomsday", this tells us that while we rest assured that pain will come again as doomsday. "Sleep on, scathed felicity. Sleep, rare and perishable relic." Here to try and sleep on scorched damaged happiness, but sleep infrequently because the past is with us and alive.

"Imagining 's no shutter against the absolute incorrigible sunrise", in existential resonance of the phoenix, I believe as long as there is a sunrise in then horrible things will continue to repeat themselves. Also addresses not to bring memory to what happened during the Holocaust, for there is assurance that the dreadful past will repeat itself.

As mesmerizing as the legend of the Phoenix fire may be, its fiery death to is viewed as a painful suffering that is relived through humanity.

The Phoenix fire has been an ancient symbol for life after death and this mythical bird's rising from the ashes depicts this idea. It is interesting to see how the phoenix fire has been adopted by various cultures and religions, despite the fact that it originated from Greek mythology. Not much is known about the history of this symbol, but we still see it today as a mystical symbol of hope against adversity.

The phrase rise like a phoenix from the ashes is based on a story that goes back thousands of years. The expression is a simile, which is a phrase used in a sentence that is a comparison of one thing with something else using the word like or the word as.

A simile may compare two things with qualities that do not seem related, though there must be some similarity that is either literal or figurative. Writers use similes in prose and in poetry as literary devices used to paint vivid imagery.

To rise like a phoenix from the ashes means to emerge from a catastrophe stronger, smarter and more powerful. An example of rising like a phoenix from the ashes is someone who opens a new, successful business after his previous business has failed.

Another example is someone who builds a new house after his previous house has been destroyed in a tornado.

REFLECT RESEARCH:

The phoenix bird is a mythical bird from Greek mythology. It was a feathered creature of great size with talons and wings, its plumage radiant and beautiful. The phoenix lived for 500 years before it built its own funeral pyre, burst into flame, and died, consumed in its own fiery inferno. Soon after, the mythical creature rose out of the ashes, in a transformation from death to life.

A counterpart to the phoenix fire is the Bennu of Egyptian mythology, which was a large heron venerated in Heliopolis, Egypt. The phoenix is a Chinese bird often depicted with fire balls.

The feathers of the Russian fire-bird emit light, and is often the subject of quests in folklore. Believer adopted the depiction of the phoenix rising from the ashes as a symbol of rebirth and eternal life. The classical, mythical imagery and symbolism of resurrection, of life reborn anew and transformed, resonated with the Believer story. Related phrases are rises like a phoenix from the ashes, rose like a phoenix from the ashes, risen like a phoenix from the ashes, rising like a phoenix from the ashes.

First, the Phoenix flew west into the mortal world.

It was necessary to come to leave Paradise and enter our world so that the creature could be reborn. It flew west until it reached the spice groves that grew in Arabia. It stopped there to collect only the finest herbs and spices (especially cinnamon) before continuing its journey to Phoenicia *(which was likely named after the creature)*. Once the Phoenix reached Phoenicia, it built a nest of the herbs and spices it had gathered and waited for the sun to rise.

The Creator began to drag his chariot across the sky, the Phoenix would turn east to face him as the sun rose above the horizon. It would then sing one of the most beautiful and haunting melodies known to man – so perfect that even the sun *The Creator* had to pause and listen to the sweet notes. When the Phoenix finished its farewell song, *The Creator* readied his chariots and continued his journey across the sky. This caused a spark to fall from the sky and ignite the nest of herbs and the Phoenix in flames. All that was left was a tiny worm.

This, however, was not the end of the cycle. After sometime had past, a new Phoenix would rise from the ashes *(supposedly*

I WAS REBORN IN THE FIRE...

transformed from the worm) and begin the next cycle of 1,000 years. It would carry the remaining ashes of its parent to the great Heliopolis and then return to Paradise until its cycle came to an end.

THOUGHTS:

Learning how to trust again.

The sun, light of the universe is constant.

It is I who moved, ran, panicked.

There is order among chaos.

There is light as well as darkness. There is Yin and Yang. I am to trust the constant, even when all else around me seems dark, when I feel unheard, when my flight or fight mentality reverts to flight. I must remember to trust in what is constant.

The sun rises in the East and sets in the West. Each day is new. Taking my head out of the sand and looking up is my second step toward spreading my wings, initiating a standing position and even considering taking on a new flight pattern in life—a new and improved way of dealing with hurt in order to love myself again.

I must find the constants in life and begin to build my trust again, even when I'm afraid, the fire will burn, so you will rise up and leave your sins and ashes behind!

THOUGHTS:

While the above tale is the most common version of the rebirth of the Phoenix, there are alternative versions that are also passed down. The first is that instead of flying to Phoenicia to end its cycle of life, the Phoenix fire flew to Heliopolis and gave itself to the fires of the sun city. From these fires, the new Phoenix emerges and then flies back to the land of Paradise.

There are also some versions where the Phoenix fire completes its journey as described above *(from Paradise to Arabia and then Phoenicia)* and then dies with the rising of the sun the next morning. The body begins to decompose (most versions of this story say this process lasts three days) and once it has reached the final

23

stages of decomposition the new Phoenix emerges from the remains of the first.

Finally, a lesser known version of the story of the Phoenix claims that the Phoenix begins to show signs of age when it reaches the final years of its lifespan. It flies to the mortal world – losing many of its beautiful feathers and lovely coloration along the way. When it finished building its nest, it sets itself on fire (similar to the first version) allowing the next Phoenix to come forward.

When the new Phoenix comes into the next cycle of life, the first thing it does is create a cremation egg to place its predecessor's remains inside. To do this, the Phoenix flies off and begins to gather the finest myrrh it can find to form into a ball. It gathers as much as it can carry and then flies back to the nest it emerged from.

Once back at its nest, the Phoenix begins to hollow out the egg of myrrh and creates a small opening on the side so that it can begin to put its predecessors' ashes inside. Once it has gathered all the ashes and put them inside the egg, it seals the opening in the cremation egg with myrrh and carries the remains back to Heliopolis. It leaves the remains on top of an alter in the temple of Ra and then begins its new life by flying back to the land of Paradise.

There are several variations on the tale of the Phoenix, but most versions say that the Phoenix resides in Paradise. This land is said to be a perfect world that was beyond the sun and was sometimes considered to be a representation of Heaven. However, there were also other versions of the story that gave other locations as residences of the Phoenix.

One location that was claimed to be the home of the Phoenix was the Heliopolis *(city of the sun)*. This may be because the Heliopolis was where the Phoenix was entombed after death. In some versions of the story, this is also where the Phoenix was reborn.

The Greeks claimed that the Phoenix was known to live next to a well in Arabia. According to their records, the Phoenix bathed itself in the well every morning at dawn and sang a song so beautiful

I WAS REBORN IN THE FIRE...

that Apollo himself *(The Creation)* had to stop his chariots in the sky to listen to the melody.

There are also several variations in the myth of the Phoenix concerning the age at which the creature is reborn. Some legends claim that the bird lives up to 1,461 years, while others claim that the bird lived for 1,000 years. Other sources estimate the bird's lifespan at a significantly smaller number.

Regardless of the version of the story that is being told, it appears that no records claim that the Phoenix dies before the age of 500 and the general cap for the life cycle of the mighty bird is typically less than 1,500 years. This can possibly be explained by the symbolism of the particular story in question and what the Phoenix was supposed to represent in the tale.

It was considered good luck in many cultures to spot a Phoenix. It was considered to signify that a good leader who was very wise had been given ruling power. It was also considered to be the sign of a new era.

The Phoenix was also known to have regenerative powers and was considered to be both invincible and immortal – excluding the end of its natural life cycle when it was necessary for the next Phoenix to be reborn. Because of this power, the Phoenix was known to be a symbol of fire and divinity that was often used by powerful leaders. The tears of the bird are also thought to have regenerative abilities that can be harnessed by humans. Additionally, new mythology concerning the Phoenix claims that it is impossible for a person to tell a lie if the creature is nearby.

RESEARCH:

The story goes as such:

There lived a large, beautiful bird with glistening feathers of red and gold which caught the attention of the Sun.

The Sun was so mesmerized by the bird's beauty, and the reflection of its own light in the bird's feathers, that the Sun laid claim on the bird and promised that the Phoenix would live forever and would belong to the Sun, himself.

The Phoenix was overjoyed to belong to the Sun and reserved the most glorious of songs to sing to the Sun each day.

However, the overwhelming beauty displayed in each of the Phoenix's feathers and the syrupy song of the Phoenix's voice was noticed and coveted by others, causing the Phoenix much distress.

One day the bird flew away to a faraway place in the East to live a life of solitude and to continue to sing songs to the Sun, who rose to greet the East every morning. Five hundred years passed. Flying freely and with a melodious song on its breath, the Phoenix began to tire.

The beloved Phoenix, in a moment of despair, sang a different song to the Sun—a song that pleaded for youth and strength. Silence. Day after day the beautiful bird sang the song, beckoning an answer from the Sun. Silence. The Phoenix considered the possibility that the Sun had not actually moved from its original spot in the sky where the original promise of immortality was given.

Perhaps if the Phoenix flew back to its home, the Sun would be there waiting to hear the new song. The journey was rigorous, as the Phoenix was weak and aged. During its many periods of rest, the bird collected spices and fragrant leaves to build a new home upon reaching its destination.

Once home again, the Phoenix collected myrrh from a nearby tree, formed an egg and placed the egg in a new nest made from the leaves and spices collected. The nest was located atop a lone tree that stood on the summit of a glorious mountain.

From this nest, the bird sang its song to the Sun, asking once again for youth and strength.

The Sun heard this new song and replied by calming the winds and chasing away the clouds and shining its intense light upon the Phoenix. All other creatures hid from the Sun's strong, luminous rays, but the Phoenix remained in its nest high on the mountain top.

I WAS REBORN IN THE FIRE...

The Sun's beam was so intense and hot, like a laser, that it consumed the Phoenix as if swallowing it whole, yet leaving the tree and the nest intact. The bird became a heap of ash in the middle of the nest and faced its own mortality.

After the mound of gray ashes had settled, there came a stirring within them. Moment by moment the ashes began to rise up out of the nest forming the shape of a bird. The Phoenix itself was reborn from its own death and completely ruined state. It rose up young and strong, brilliant and beautiful again, just as it had requested in its song to the Sun.

Once again, the Phoenix sang its praises to the Sun before flying off to a land far away to reside alone with the Sun. Every 500 years when the Phoenix began losing strength and youth, it would fly back to its nest where death to self, resurrection and renewal would occur once again.

The phoenix fire is the reputation of our new life and renew power…It is the symbol

RESEARCH:

The story begins in the days when people were still allowed in the Garden of Eden. It is said that when Eve gave into the temptations of the serpent and tempted Adam with the fruit, she also offered the fruit to the other animals in the garden. The Milcham bird was among the animals that refused to partake of the fruit and was therefore rewarded for its faithfulness. It was given a town where it could live its days out in peace eternally. Every 1,000 years, the Milcham bird would end one cycle of life, but being immune to the Angel of Death *(because it had remained faithful to The Creation)* it would be reborn again.

REFLECT:

The Slavic Fire bird has obvious ties to the Phoenix fire and was likely created in their folklore when the ancient cultures exchanged stories and legends on their trade routes. However, unlike many other cultures who told of the Phoenix, the Firebird was depicted as a giant falcon instead of a peacock.

It is thought that this is because the falcon symbolized ultimate masculinity in the Slavic culture.

The Slavic Fire bird was also different from the traditional Phoenix because of its life cycle. Their Fire bird was meant to symbolize the different seasons. The bird finishes its life cycle in the fall months but is revived again in the spring. With its revival comes beautiful music that brings happiness and new life.

NOTICE:

The myth of the Phoenix was not only common in ancient mythology, it was also adopted by several religions and was sometimes used to represent theoretical ideas and the reign of powerful kingdoms. The element of rebirth in the story has often been used to describe a wide range of ideas.

Although the Phoenix fire was known as Bennu in ancient Egypt, the two mythical creatures have been identified as the same entity. In Egypt, however, the sign of the solar bird was used to symbolize of rebirth and immortality. The story of Bennu's rebirth was thought to closely follow the rebirth of the human spirit as well.

The story of the Phoenix has also been hypothesized as a possible way of retelling *The Creator* of the earth. Because the Phoenix is so closely related to the sun, there are some who would hypothesize that the birth of the Phoenix could also be the birth of a new world. This birth would result from a cosmic fire that could be symbolized by the bright colors of the Phoenix's feathers, as well as the flames from which it arises.

When exploring this version of the story, it is often concluded that the death of the Phoenix describes the death of a world or galaxy through the explosion of its sun. However, this explosion is not the end of life, as it makes way for a new world to be created.

In Greek mythology, it is often thought that the story of the

Phoenix is used to describe a philosophical term called 'metempsychosis.' This reflected the spiritual beliefs of many who lived in Ancient Greece.

Metempsychosis is known to be 'the transmigration of the soul.' This is the process in which the spirit of a person is reincarnated after death. The use of the Phoenix to symbolize this belief helps to explain that the soul of a person never really dies.

It is simply transformed and rebirthed into another life as it moves from a person's body in death and back to the Earth when it is ready to enter a new life cycle.

There has always been much speculation into the inspiration of a creature as impressive as the Phoenix. Some hypothesize that the flamingo of East Africa could have served for at least part of the inspiration of the tale.

It is known that the flamingo of East Africa lives in an area that is too hot for its young to survive. Because of this, it has to build a mound of earthen materials in order to elevate its nest so that the eggs and hatchlings can survive the heat. It is said that the convection currents around the mounds created by this bird are similar to the movement of a flame – which could have been why the Phoenix was associated with fire.

RESEARCH:

Life From The Ashes Of The Frames

The phoenix, by reputation, is closely associated with the sun. The symbol often depicts a large red bird rising up from a fire. This is because the phoenix symbolizes life after death or hope after destruction. The phoenix can represent many beliefs such as:
• The soul goes on after death
• Out of troubled circumstances comes eventual good
• Hope never dies
• Beauty out of the ashes
It is for this reason that some religions throughout the ages adopted

this symbol, as will be seen further below. Although it is no longer the case, in early Believer history, the symbol of the phoenix was adopted by some Believer churches to portray spiritual life after death. Believers believe that people are 'born again' after repenting of their sins, and so their bodies are considered dead and replaced by new spiritual life. It may also have been a symbol of life after death, in that the soul lives on after the body has died.

The symbol is more likely to be seen in a tattoo parlor than a church nowadays. Mysticism and spiritualism have adopted the symbol now and it is simply representative of rising above hardship. It is seen now as purely mythological and yet the idea of a phoenix rising from the fiery ashes is an attractive one for many.

The phoenix itself is likely to feature in animated shows, video games, and adventure books.

The ashes are the reputation of our sins...

We can still learn something valuable from the symbol of the phoenix. Our lives are filled with hardship and challenges and a philosophy stating that we can rise above those circumstances—no matter how bad they become—is a good mind set to have.

So, the next time you see the phoenix, remember what it stands for, remember where it comes from, and remember where it has been throughout history.

REFLECT THOUGHTS:

If you have phoenix dreams, you are lucky indeed.

While many of us have animal dreams, few of us dream of mythical animals.

Dream meanings and interpretations are personal to every individual. However, one thing we all have in common is that our subconscious emotions don't lie to us. Analyzing the emotions, you felt in your dream can provide clues into what the dream is telling you.

While dreams about animals can be interpreted in any number of ways, as a mythical animal, the phoenix has very specific meanings. In general, a dream about a phoenix can be viewed as an opportunity for transformation, renewal, and continuity.

We might get the feeling that we need to be baptized again. Many times, we get that feeling because of some sin or doubt we're wrestling. We may feel like we can lose our salvation when we mess up, and therefore we need to start the whole process over.

However, that's not what salvation and baptism are about.

Baptism is a one-time symbol of a one-time salvation.

If your baptism came after you decided to follow *The Creation*, that was the right time to be baptized. It's a public expression of your new direction with *The Creation*.

If salvation depended on us, we would be in trouble; but by The Creator's grace, it doesn't. *The Creator* brought spiritual cleansing for all through His death on the cross and resurrection from the tomb.

Taking steps with *The Creator* is a daily process. He doesn't require us to be perfect or have it all together. He wants to help you make progress and He's with you for the long haul.

To rise like a phoenix from the ashes means to emerge from a catastrophe stronger, smarter and more powerful. An example of rising like a phoenix from the ashes is someone who opens a new, successful business after his previous business has failed. ... The phoenix bird is a mythical bird from Greek mythology.

Why can't we live happily ever after and skip all the negative parts of life?

If only someone could give us the perfect answer for this. But the truth is that nothing we say or do can stop this type of inquiry because having a life without struggle, pain, and suffering is only possible in our heads.

The perfect life is a combination of both ups and downs. Everything has its reverse, and we'll always see that throughout our lives. It is necessary to have both ups and downs because the downs in our lives keep us grounded and kind.

The ups make us feel blessed and inspire us to show a little gratitude to the people around us. Having a life without ups and downs would be plain and boring. You might be sighing about this idea, but it is true.

When you can acknowledge and appreciate both the ups and downs, you'll be able to cultivate greater contentment and inner harmony. If you listen closely to yourself and pay attention to your mood, you'll notice that you experience many slight ups and downs on a daily basis. It's a simple fact of life.

These ups and downs can bring us closer to the parts of ourselves that need attention, validation, and love and make us feel grateful for whatever we have in our lives. Having both of these things in our lives helps us to stay grounded.

Imagine a roller coaster: it's impossible to separate the ups and the downs from each other.
Both are necessary for an exciting and complete experience. Similarly, life is one big roller coaster, with the ups and downs both essential for creating a whole and enjoyable life. Having ups and downs makes us human.

No matter how much we repeat that it's normal to have ups and downs, some of us have a hard time handling them. Most of us have trouble maintaining balance during both good times and bad. However, it is possible to learn how to handle the ups and downs. As we've described, ups and downs are inextricably linked, and you cannot have one without the other.

But being low doesn't have to lead to depression, self-doubt, or self-judgment. And the upward spiral doesn't have to lead to excessive elation, ego, or satisfaction.

When you realize that you are going through hard times and the things you love aren't exciting anymore, take a step back and just try to breathe. Remind yourself that it will pass. All the bad things that are happening to you are momentary and temporary. Soon you

I WAS REBORN IN THE FIRE...

will be in a better place, where you don't feel like this anymore.

We understand that this often doesn't make any sense to someone who may be suffering, but when practiced, it is helpful. Our heart is like a kid who needs to be consoled from time to time. The reminder that it's not going to be like this forever will bring you some relief.

PRAYER:

I bow my knee before you, O Father, from whom every family in heaven and on earth is named, that according to the riches of your glory you may grant me to be strengthened with might through your Spirit in the inner man.

The Creator may dwell in my heart through faith; that, being rooted and grounded in love, I might have power to comprehend with all the saints what is the breadth and length and height and depth and to know the love of The Creator which passes knowledge, that I might be filled with all the fullness of The Creator.

RESEARCH:

Paul doesn't say that all have fallen short of the glory of *The Creation.* Look at the verb tense here: all fall short of the glory of *The Creation.* He shifts to the present tense for a reason.

We often use Romans 3:23 to show the unbeliever that he has sinned and that he falls short of the glory of *The Creation.*

Actually, the verse says that all have sinned and all fall short of the glory of *The Creation.*

That includes each and every believer as well!

Believer, you right now fall short of the glory of *The Creation.* Until you die or are raptured, you will continue to fall short of the glory of *The Creation.* The most mature saint still falls short of the glory of *The Creation.* Here is were a teeth age would not truth understand, but life is good but when some of us hit that wall we can lost our way in this world. Haven't we all felt the same at one point or the other in life. It's just a part of life to lose your way, to take a break and to reconnect with yourself.

First, you need to get to know yourself - the real you, not the you have tried to be. Stop trying to be another herd animal and start thinking for yourself. Discover your limits and then push them.

Consider your options and make a choice then move forward. Make the best choice you can see to make at the time and go with it. If it doesn't work out, try something else, but don't regret any choice you made if it was the best you could see to make at the time you made it. The worst decisions you can ever make is to do nothing and to stop putting one foot in front of the other moving forward. Choosing not to choose is a choice.

Consider a 40-year-old paraplegic who had lived an active life and suddenly lost the use of his legs. He is lost. He can either embrace his new life, learn to be independent and move forward, or he can choose to do nothing and live out his life as a cripple.

No matter how he deals with it he has to make a choice.

The alcoholic who has been sober twice in the past year, on Thanksgiving and Christmas.

He lost his job and his family and his home, lives on the street and in shelters and eats only in the soup kitchen. He works as a day laborer and panhandles to get money to buy his booze. He is lost. He can continue to be lost, leave alcohol in charge of his life, drink himself into an early grave; or he can take charge of his own life, seek treatment for his addiction, find a steady job, get a new home and perhaps regain his family or start a new one. Either way, he and he alone can make the choice. If he ends up in an early grave from alcoholism it is not because he was lost, but because he chose to remain lost.

I sat down on the floor that night like a when my mom passed away. In this case, no one was dead but I was grieving.

Uncontrollable steams of tears went down my face.

I sat there shaking in anger and talking to *The Creator*, pouring out all my emotions before *The Creation*. I asked *The Creator*

I WAS REBORN IN THE FIRE...

why He would let me go through something so painful. I yelled at *The Creator* for allowing me to go through pain.

I was broken, so broken that I couldn't see any glimmer of hope. All I thought of, dwelled on were negative thoughts. And the more I allowed negativity into my heart, the more I felt hopeless.

Five Strategies For Dealing With The Pain of Life

Here are five practices that will help you deal more easily with the ups and downs of life.

Practice kindness – Generally, when we're going through a hard time, we forget to be kind to ourselves. We force ourselves to carry on as if everything is fine and then burden ourselves with unnecessary guilt.

Know that it is natural if you don't want to do any chores or go to work on your hard days. Just look out for yourself and try to be kind to yourself.

Don't let fear rule your life – It's crucial not to let your fear dictate how you live your life.

Fear creates a barrier that prevents your growth. Instead, face your fears and work to overcome them, break down that barrier and create a way through to a more peaceful state.

Allow healing into your life – Let healing come to you. Healing is not something rare or fancy.
As we've already said, be kind to yourself, and accept opportunities for healing and growth. Do things that make you feel good about yourself and your existence.

Believe in the universe – Maintaining a positive perspective or believing in the universe providing what you need will help you get through the negative times.

So, have faith that whatever is happening to you is for your good.

Reach out to people – When it is too much for you to handle, one of the best things you can do is reach out to people who can help you.

They can be professionals, or friends, or family. Do you know that one out of every eight adults seek mental health care?

Let the stats give you the strength to reach out to a therapist. Talking about suffering, pain, or trauma is okay, and you don't need to feel ashamed and hide it from the world.

Understand that sleepless nights are going to happen, and sometimes you're going to need to let go and have a good cry. This is all part of moving through tough times, and all of us will have to deal with many tough times throughout our lives.

There is no way out but through. Finding courage and having faith that you can deal with life's ups and downs is the answer. Simply put, dealing with everything that life throws at you is living, so embrace it.

This is a difficult process and one that can only be done once the standing up position has been accomplished. Sin, hurt and pain, self-inflicted or by others, holds a strong position in life.

It can become this larger-than-life entity that is all consuming, all powerful and completely destructive. It is driven by fear which is also a larger-than-life entity that can be all-encompassing.

Going back to one's roots takes courage and can truly only be accomplished from the standing up position of bravery, where we meet our pain eye to eye and disallow fear to crumble us. It's a conscious decision to stand up like a wall and provide a fortress around your heart and meet your life-killing adversary head on!

How?

Well, for me it helped to watch or listen to empowering, motivational videos to boost my confidence and give me a fist-first mentality. List to positive music rather than listening to the music that weakens the spirit. Simultaneously conquer a tangible goal to enable facing the inner demons that haunt. Do things that are scary to build up confidence and tear down fear.

I WAS REBORN IN THE FIRE...

This path is can take you to the dark or the light side.

Live your life with conviction, purpose and live it vibrantly! Baptism is a public symbol of our decision to trust and follow *The Creation*. In a moment, it showed what *The Creator* did for us, and now we get to see how that plays out in every part of our lives.

Your number one goal from this point forward is to listen to *The Creator* and do what Holy Spirit says. It's nothing fancy or really complicated, but it's the best way to move forward.

It's a spiritual impossibility to follow *The Creator* and remain the same. As we listen to Him and do what He says, we will see how it's true that growing people change.

The changes aren't from our own ideas or strength, but by the guidance of the Holy Spirit—that's the spirit of *The Creator* living inside us. He's the one who gives us the power to love and forgive others, to grow in faith, and to say no to sin and yes to *The Creation*. These kinds of qualities will continue to show up more and more in our lives as we seek *The Creation*.

The truth is we won't have all the answers automatically. Our lives won't instantaneously be cleaned up and easy, but that's not the point—a relationship with *The Creators* the point. Our public step in baptism is just the beginning of the changes *The Creator* will bring us through.

Baptism is a picture of death, burial, and resurrection. It means going public with our faith in *The Creator* and symbolizes that once we come out of the water, we are not the person we were when entering in. We are no longer defined by our sin, but brought to new life with *The Creator* like He resurrected into new life.

Think of it like a ring symbolizes marriage. If you take your wedding ring off, you are no less married; however, with it on, it shows the rest of the world that you are committed in a relationship unlike anything else.

NOTICE:

You have been made new in your salvation, and baptism is a symbol to those watching—and to those you tell later—that you are no longer a slave to sin and death but are alive in *The Creator*. Because of *The Creator* everyone can live in freedom.

REFLECT:

In your own words and including your personal story, how would you explain what baptism means? Share this with a friend or family member today.

Many people think the question Nicodemus poses shows that he is a rather dimwitted literalist. But that's almost certainly too harsh. You don't get to be called "the teacher of Israel" (John 3:10—possibly a title) if you can't spot the odd metaphor.

When you hears *The Creator* say that to enter the kingdom one must be "born again," I suspect Nicodemus understands *The Creator* to mean that we are not good enough to enter the kingdom: we must start over, have a different origin, spring from a different life. Nicodemus thinks *The Creators* going too far: people can't really start over or claim a new life, boast of a new birth, or enjoy a new beginning.

This is being may be reborn as the phoenix is reborn thought the fire by the power of the creator and the ashes of our sins are blowing in the wind.

Most of us have faced moments when we wish we could "start over," or at least expunge some of our worst sins and faults. "Oh, for a man to arise in me That the man I am may no longer be,"

RESEARCH:

"If life had a second edition, how I would correct the proofs." Nicodemus perceives the futility of insisting that we must have a new beginning: it's a bit late to demand a new beginning when we've made such a mess of the voyage (John 3:4, 9). And if that's what is required to get into the kingdom, there is no hope:

"How can someone be born when they are old?"

This is where many may be reborn as the phoenix is reborn thought the flames by the power of the creator and the ashes of our sins are blowing in the wind.

But far from backing down, *The Creator* repeats the point (John 3:5), yet he does so in such a way that he expands on "born again," turning it into "born of water and the Spirit," and thus provides some explanation. That's why it is so important to understand what *The Creator* means by this expression.

Several suggestions have been put forward that turn out to be rather unsatisfactory. Some propose that *The Creators* specifying two to three births: one must undergo not only natural birth ("born of water") but also spiritual birth ("born of . . . the Spirit"). People must not only be born, but must be born "again." There are two primary problems with this interpretation: It is unbearably trite. The first part is saying not much more than that to get into the kingdom, you must exist: you must be born, you must be here.

That means all the weight of *The Creator's* answer is carried in the second part, "born of . . . the Spirit," making us wonder what the first part, "born of water," is contributing to The Creator's explanation.

No one can see the kingdom of *The Creation*, no one can enter the kingdom of *The Creator*, unless they are born again, unless they are born of water and the Spirit. Immediately it becomes clear that "born of water and the Spirit" (3:5) is parallel to "born again" (3:5). In other words, "born of water and the Spirit" can't refer to two births, one natural and one spiritual; rather, it refers to one birth, the birth *The Creators* referring to when he speaks of being "born again." It follows that *The Creation's* use of "born of water and the Spirit" is *The Creation's* explanation of what he means by "born again," and is intended to answer Nicodemus's question.

Second, in what follows it becomes apparent that *The Cre-*

ator thinks his explanation should have been enough for Nicodemus. Indeed, *The Creator* rebukes Nicodemus for not understanding, even though he is "the teacher of Israel" (3:9–10). As a learned Pharisee, Nicodemus had studied what we would call the Old Testament, along with a great deal of additional theological reflection. From all this learning, what should Nicodemus have picked up from *The Creation's* words that should have given him much better understanding of what *The Creator* was talking about?

That brings us to the third detail, the decisive clue.

The question to ask is this: where do "water" and "the Spirit" come together in the Old Testament in a context that promises a new beginning?

There are several possibilities,

But the most obvious is Ezekiel 36:25–27:

I will sprinkle clean water upon you, and you will be clean. I will cleanse you from all your impurities and from all your idols.

I will give you a new heart and put a new spirit in you; I will remove from you your heart of stone and give you a heart of flesh. And I will put my Spirit in you and move you to follow my decrees and be careful to keep my laws.

So, *The Creators* promising through the prophet Ezekiel, six centuries before *The Creation,* that a time is coming when there will be a transformative new beginning, characterized by spectacular cleansing symbolized by water that washes away all impurities and idols, and by the powerful gift of the Spirit that transforms the hearts of people. That is what is required if people are to see and enter the kingdom of *The Creation.*

Fourth, with a little more space it would be possible to show how this interpretation of the words "born of water and the Spirit" coheres with the rest of the passage, and indeed with the Gospel of John. *The Creator* happily insists that this declaration of the need for this kind of new birth has behind it the authority of revelation: he himself has come from heaven to bring it (3:11–13). And the pat-

I WAS REBORN IN THE FIRE...

tern of *The Creator* reaching down and powerfully saving his people from their sin and idolatry is already there in the Old Testament (3:14–15; cf. Num. 21:4–9).

Indeed, all of this is grounded in the matchless love of *The Creator* (John 3:16–21), and is accessible to faith: "For *The Creator* so loved the world that he gave his one and only Son, that whoever believes in him shall not perish but have eternal life" (John 3:16).

QUESTIONS:

Baptism is an outward expression of an inward change. It's a public declaration of how *The Creator* changed your life. Being baptized shows others that you've decided to follow *The Creation*, and allows them to celebrate this decision with you. (I Corinthians 15:3-4, Colossians 2:12)

Baptism doesn't make you a believer - it shows that you already believe. Baptism doesn't "save" you, only your faith in *The Creator* does that. Baptism is like a wedding ring - it's the outward symbol.

Why Should I Be Baptized?

The Creator instructs us to be baptized and set the example by being baptized (Matthew 28:19-20, Mark 1:9).

Obedience to *The Creator* shows we believe and follow Him. (1 John 2:3). Because *The Creator* went public about His love for us, we can go public about our love for Him. Being baptized shows that we turn away from a life of sin toward *The Creation*, the only one who can change us (Acts 2:38-41).

When's The Best Time To Be Baptized?

For everyone who decides to follow *The Creation*, baptism is the next step. Anyone who commits his or her life to following *The Creators* ready to be baptized (Acts 8:12).

NOTICE:

What About Infant Baptism?

At Connecting Point, we wait until our children are old enough to believe and understand the true meaning of baptism, and old enough to remember their baptism, before we baptize them.

Some churches practice infant baptism. This ceremony is similar in nature to our practice of child dedication, and is intended to be a covenant between the parents and *The Creator* on the behalf of the child—the parents promise to raise their child in the faith until the child is old enough to make his own personal confession of *The Creation*. The custom of infant baptism began about 300 years after the Bible was completed.

Infant baptism is not a practice found in Scripture, nor do we find evidence of its practice by the early church.

The biblical purpose for baptism is to publicly profess your personal commitment to *The Creation*

The phoenix bird symbolizes immortality, resurrection and life after death, and in ancient Greek and Egyptian mythology it is associated with the sun *The Creation*. ...

Only one phoenix exists at a time, and so when the bird felt its death was near, every 500 to 1,461 years, it would build a nest of aromatic wood and set it on fire.

Salvation and baptism are milestones in your walk with *The Creation*.

But what now?

What do you do when your next step is just to make it through a regular day?

Following *The Creator* on a daily basis can seem like a far-off goal that's hard to attain. *The Creator* doesn't expect us to walk blindly through our days hoping that we get it right. He has given us the Holy Spirit and His words in the Bible as a guide so we can know what He wants us to do.

The Bible was given to us to train and teach us how to follow *The Creation*. As we read it, we learn more about who *The Creators*, who we are, and how we can make decisions that obey Him. When

I WAS REBORN IN THE FIRE...

we are walking in obedience, we most clearly see *The Creator's* plan for our lives. He wants better things for us and the only way to get there is to follow His directions.

The Creators calling you to do good things. He uses the Bible to equip us to do what He's called us to do. The more we read His Word, the more we learn to live in connection with *The Creation.*

REFLECT:

Baptism is going public in saying that The Creators Lord of your life.

When you asked *The Creator* for help, for healing, and for salvation, you claimed the promise that He will never let you down. *The Creator* stands by His promise to save you, change you, and stay with you.

The Creator's promise applies, no matter who you are or what you've done. Saying yes to *The Creators* accepting the salvation He freely gives.

NOTICE:

Being saved by *The Creator* means you've been rescued.

No more trying to live up to someone's expectations, no more hiding in shame, no more attempts to fix your own life. *The Creator* rescues you from all of that. Going public is about showing on the outside how *The Creators* changing you on the inside.

Every time *The Creator* makes a difference in your life, it deserves a celebration. He is only getting started with you, and the best is yet to come.

REFLECT:

Our problems aren't automatically fixed, but The Creator promises to be with us and help us through them.

You made a public statement of your faith when you were baptized, and now you get to walk with *The Creator* as a continued daily "yes," affirming to *The Creation*, yourself, and those around you that you have been made new.

The difference now is that you aren't trying to build up yourself; you're built up by *The Creation*.

Just as you said "yes" to *The Creation*, now you get to keep saying yes to Him. No matter what happens, we can have peace in *The Creation*: "In this world you will have trouble. But take heart! I have overcome the world" (John 16:33). The Bible promises that the same *The Creator* who saved you is the *The Creator* who sustains and rescues you (Isaiah 46:4).

Be overflowing with gratitude at this bold next step of faith that you have taken, knowing a life with *The Creators* a life of continual growth. It's a life of next steps.

Sometimes we change in a moment, but often it takes time. Be patient, trusting in *The Creator's* perfect timing and provision.

Reflect: Now that you've been baptized, what questions you have? Contact the host you've already talked with or get in touch with someone on the Care Team today.

In the harrowing aftermath of a major wildfire, it may be difficult to appreciate the restorative power in the fire itself. Especially when nothing remains to hold the land in place once the rain comes, resulting in flash flooding and mud slides.

But the rain and fire also breathes life back into the remaining landscape, allowing new vegetation to grow in the charred areas. Seeds stored in the forest floor begin to germinate. Some trees begin to sprout branches from basal buds of dead trees.

And some species even rely upon wildfire for propagation. For instance, the seeds of jack pines and lodge pole pines are sealed by a resinous bond which can only be cracked open by the high temperatures associated with wildfire.

The phoenix is reborn thought the flames by the power of the creator and the ashes are our sins.

THOUGHTS:

I WAS REBORN IN THE FIRE...

When your world comes crashing down, you have a chance to do something you couldn't have done before: rise up.

You can only be reborn if you've known what it feels like to die inside.

Your story might be called "Resilience" or "Hope" or even "Freedom." It's the story of the phoenix.

Suffering changes you. If you let it, what happens to you becomes fuel for something new. It's a teacher you learn how to not run away from. If you can do that (and you can), you'll learn how to live through what you thought would destroy you.

Falling apart gives you a reason to build something new.

One thing that helps?

Sharing your story. Telling your truth. It's a healing, not only for you but for those who want to know how they, too, can rise from the ashes of destruction.

How many times do you rise after you've come crashing down?

Every single time.

If you're ready to see how you can take your pain and give back differently, read these phoenix quotes. They'll give you a glimpse of what's possible when it seems like nothing's left.

Believe in your ability to rise from your own fallen ashes to become brighter and more beautiful than ever before. You can do that.

You were born for that.

RESEARCH:

The Dark Frames of the phoenix were considered by the the inter self to be the element aligned with selfishness, fear, hatred, aggression, and malice toward all living things. Such emotions seemed to increase the strength and abilities of a user of the sin within, providing a path towards personal power and the destruction or control of all opposition. It was generally accepted that use of the dark frames was extremely addictive. We all have the choose that choose can save you or take your very soul.

Despite the progression of civilization and society's attempts to suppress man's darker side, moral depravity proves both indestructible and inescapable; contrary to culturally embraced views of humanistic tendencies towards goodness, each individual is susceptible to his base, innate instincts.

NOTICE:

The power to manipulate the dark/destructive aspects of fire. Variation of Dark Element Manipulation. Combination of Fire Manipulation,Negative Forces Manipulation And Destructive Energy Manipulation Opposite to Pure Fire … Dark fire is volatile/destructive, causing harm to oneself/environment by accident is ever-present danger. Distance, mass, precision, etc. Depend upon of the knowledge, skill, and strength of the user, and their power's natural limits.

THOUGHTS:

Human nature, it is the characteristics that all of mankind portrays through its behavior. Thus showing mankind's true colors or in other words the truth about itself. In essence, the truth within human nature there is aspects such as curiosity and fear, it could lead man to develop traits such as avarice and prejudice or worst of all temptation. These aspects of human nature can all come with a lack of understanding when faced with enigma's. All of these traits inherited from humanity's ancestors

However, held the belief that mankind is naturally evil and that society needs an absolute central authority to contain this evilness and grant its people with the common protection.

Many believes that in a state of nature, when there are no rules and everyone is granted equal power, the inherent evil impulses of man are exposed.

The symbol of fire (Phoenix) has always stood for life, love

I WAS REBORN IN THE FIRE…

and health, for energy, transformation and regeneration, for light and warmth. When we feel passion for something or someone, we feel the fiery heat of an enkindled inner flame. We burn with it, that fire of inner feeling, and it sustains us. This is being of the phoenix is reborn thought the fire by the power of the creator and the ashes of our sins are blowing in the wind.

The Romans used the phoenix symbol on their coins to represent both rebirth and the imperishable existence of the empire. Clement of Rome in the First Epistle of Clement to the Corinthians makes the earliest known connection of the tale of the phoenix to the fact of the resurrection.

When you walk through the fire I sat down on the floor that night like a person sitting down to mourn in a house in sitting room/ upper room where someone just passed away. In my case, no one was dead but I was grieving.

Uncontrollable steams of tears went down my face.

I sat there shaking in anger and talking to *The Creation,* pouring out all my emotions before Him. I asked Him why He would let me go through something so painful. I yelled at Him for allowing me to go through pain.

I was broken, so broken that I couldn't see any glimmer of hope. All I thought of, dwelled on were negative thoughts. And the more I allowed negativity into my heart, the more I felt hopeless.

Later that night after having several battles with my mind, trying to focus on the positives and trying to sleep, I felt *The Creator* was bringing a scripture to my mind. It is the scripture that says "When you pass through the waters, I will be with you; And through the rivers, they shall not overflow you. When you walk through the fire, you shall not be burned, Nor shall the flame scorch you." (Isaiah 43:2, NJKV)

REFLECT THOUGHTS:
Let the sin die...The only way to do this is to let it go. After

facing it at its roots, standing up to it, one must allow a death of that part of self to occur.

The phoenix built a nest much like the piles of ash that I swept into the darkened corners of my heart. I, along with the phoenix, felt safe there because I had been the one to build a place for my sin to live…thinking that I could control its dreadful spread into other parts of my life.

However, I was wrong.

The sin had to die in order to end its path of destruction.

I had to die to that part of myself. I had to let it go.

This is a process.

It takes time, great strength and endurance.

It is tiring and causes even more pain to rise to the surface. There are tears and anguish…a ripping away of self. It is scary moving out of the self-made coping mechanisms *(a nest that does not actually work)* and allowing oneself to be consumed in the fire of truth, honesty, vulnerability.

It feels like a burning flame that could destroy all of self.

But once the scorching is complete and the hot-white flame of purification and purging has done its work—and oh what a beautifully new creature emerges.

What stuck out to me in this scripture is the use of 'when' not 'if'. *The Creator* doesn't say, "if you walk through the fire". He says 'when you walk through the fire." 'If' would mean I may or may not walk through the fire.

'When' means I will definitely walk through the fire.

As I meditated on this scripture I realized that times of walking through the fire are inevitable. I cannot evade it. You cannot evade it. There are hard seasons when we feel like the world is crashing on us and *The Creator* has forgotten about us.

There are seasons of pain, brokenness, and struggles. But this is what *The Creator* says: "When you walk through the fire, you shall not be burned, Nor shall the flame scorch you." That flame is

I WAS REBORN IN THE FIRE…

not meant to burn you. It is meant to purify you.

As someone who cooks a lot, I know the dangers and the strengths of fire. Fire can burn you but also, fire can make delicious food happen. It is because of the heat in my kitchen that I am able to cook, to grill, to fry, to sauté and bake.

Fire/heat makes tasty things happen.

So, do you feel the phoenix flames inside you?

You need that flames of fire to build you into the person *The Creator* wants you to be. The flames is not there to burn you but to prepare you. It is there to help you build character. It is there to build resilience. It is there to make your faith stronger.

And most importantly, note that *The Creators* right there with you. As you walk through the flames, as you go through difficulties and question why. As your heart aches in pain. As you cry so many tears that leave you with swollen eyes.

As you struggle to find rest at night but sleep evades you, know that He is there, close enough. You will walk through this flames and come out better, strengthened than ever before.

As I realized this that night, I stopped being mad at *The Creator* and felt peace instead. And I found myself being thankful for something I never thought I will be thankful for, which is trials.

Yes, I am thankful for trying moments because they are building moments.

Just remember: "When you pass through the waters, I will be with you; And through the rivers, they shall not overflow you.

When you walk through the fire, you shall not be burned, Nor shall the flame scorch you." Isaiah 43:2, NKJV

How fires bring on new life?

For example, when a fire burns through bushland, it clears thick undergrowth and opens up the canopy so sunlight can reach the forest floor, encouraging the germination and regrowth of native vegetation. ...

NOTICE RESEARCH:

Research shows bush fires help provide nutrients that native vegetation specifically needs to rejuvenate and seed.

Some Believers believe that we should desire a baptism of fire based upon Bible verses that seem to show The Creator purifying and cleansing his people. Is this interpretation correcting? The Scripture in question is in the book of Matthew.

John the Baptist is at the Jordan river preaching repentance and offering baptism to those in Jerusalem, Judea and the surrounding area who came to hear him (Matthew 3:5). Although some came out of a sincere desire to hear the truth, others came for selfish reasons (verse 7 - 8).

John's response to the self-righteous religious leaders who came to hear him was to mention a fire baptism that will be carried out by *The Creation!*

John stated that *The Creator* would soon, ". . . baptize you with the Holy Spirit, and with fire" (Matthew 3:11, HBFV). Notice that two baptisms are mentioned. The first one occurs when someone repents of their sins, accepts Our lord as their Savior, and they receive *The Creator's* Spirit which makes them a true believer.

Although most religious leaders were initially against the gospel some of them later repented (Acts 6:7).

John's continues his discussion by scolding and warning the leaders of what will happen to those who refuse to repent.

Using symbolic language, he warns that those who are considered "chaff" will receive a unique baptism not of water but of fire! Verse 12 of Matthew 3 states, "Whose winnowing shovel is in His hand, and He will thoroughly purge His floor, and will gather His wheat into the granary; but the chaff He will burn up with unquenchable fire."

Verse 12 of Matthew 3 uses the same dual comparison as verse 11. *The Creator* will first collect HIS wheat and put it into his granary, which corresponds to the "good" baptism of verse 11.

I WAS REBORN IN THE FIRE...

The chaff, however, corresponds to the second group of people who will be burnt up in unquenchable fire.

How can we, however, verify that this is a correction interpretation?

In Matthew 13 *The Creator* gave a parable about a man who discovered his enemy had secretly planted weeds among his good wheat seeds.

When the man's servants asked him, what should be done he states, "Allow both to grow together until the harvest . . . (then) gather the tares first, and bind them into bundles to burn them; but gather the wheat into my granary." (Matthew 13:30).

The Creator interprets his parable of Matthew 13:24 - 30 for us a few verses later when he states the wheat or good seed symbolizes those who will ultimately be in *The Creator's* kingdom (verses 37 - 38). The tares (weeds(sins), however, are the unrepentant who will be receive a baptism of fire - meaning they will soon be burned up (verses 38, 40).

RESEARCH:

Some professing Believers who think that a baptism of or by fire is a good thing believe 'the floor' mentioned by John the Baptist in Matthew 3:12 represents individual believer who have their sins burned away or purged. *The Creation*, according to this belief, uses his 'fan' or 'winnowing shovel' to stoke up flames meant to purge a believer's "chaff" or "dross" (their sins) out of their lives and leaving only "the wheat" or good part.

This interpretation, however, is simply not correct.

The wheat that remains he gathers up for his granary. What John preached in Matthew 3 and the parable *The Creato*r gave in Matthew 13 OVERLAP regarding how *The Creator* will ultimately judge humans by one of two baptisms.

The wheat of both Matthew 3:12 and *The Creator'* parable in Matthew 13 represent true believer.

The chaff (Matthew 3:12) or tares (13:25 - 30) are unrepentant people deceived by Satan the devil. They, for a time, are allowed to exist alongside the righteous. When the moment of *The Creator's* judgment comes, he will separate the wheat (righteous) from the chaff or tares (those who refuse to repent). The righteous will be allowed entrance into *The Creator's* Kingdom.

REFLECT:

What will happen to the chaff or tares?

They will receive a baptism of fire, meaning that they will be burnt up and destroyed forever in a lake filled with it (Revelation 20:14, Malachi 4:1)! It is definitely something a person should not desire!

"I love the way they chose to take care of themselves, that they didn't fall into the grave and just die — that they made a choice that they were goanna rise like a phoenix from the ashes."

'For just as the phoenix is reborn of its dead self, so again the spiritual nature of man will rise triumphant from its dead physical body.' That is also the reason why the phoenix is a symbol of alchemical transmutation equivalent to human regeneration.

In fact, one of the secret alchemical formulae was named the Phoenix.

RESEARCH:

Call upon a Phoenix when you are distressed or feeling hopeless. This will help you understand the endless cycle of life followed by death, followed by life. The phoenix will give you courage, hope, and also instill in you a sense of rebirth and renewal.

The phoenix and its nest burn furiously and are reduced to ashes, from which a new, young phoenix (new spirit) arises.

If the phoenix is your power animal, then you are receiving a message from the other realm – a message of renewal, rebirth, immortality, and transformation.

You are always scanning the horizon, collecting information

I WAS REBORN IN THE FIRE...

about your environment, and even about your death.

You are independent and probably an introvert as well. You like singing soulful and haunting melodies and frankincense and myrrh make you feel calm and rejuvenated.

Meditate upon the Phoenix and find out what it is trying to tell you. You can light a red candle and observe its flame. Then try and seek your inner flame – the flame within- the flame of hope, renewal, and immortality.

Do not be afraid of changes or death – for death is certainly not the end.

But there must be a beginning. Nobody by nature delights so much in the character of *The Creator* that he hungers after the true *The Creation*. We are by nature children of wrath (Ephesians 2:3). As David said in Psalm 51:5, "Behold, I was brought forth in iniquity and in sin did my mother conceive me."

We come into the world bent on being independent from *The Creator* and loving the things of the world. Something has to happen to us if we are to be saved from the wrath of *The Creator* (1 Thessalonians 1:10). We must be profoundly changed.

The Bible speaks of this change in many different ways. I'll mention a few. We must change slave masters; we must cease from being slaves of sin and become slaves of *The Creator* (Romans 6:17–23). We must die with Our lord and rise to newness of life (Romans 6:3, 4; Galatians 2:20; Colossians 2:12).

We must put off the old soul and put on the new soul created after the likeness of *The Creator* (Ephesians 4:22–24; Colossians 3:9, 10). We must repent, that is, we must experience a change of mind that causes us to turn from trusting man to trusting The Creator's mercy (Acts 2:38; Luke 3:3, 8).

I will give them a new heart and put a new spirit within them; I will take the stony heart out of their flesh and give them a heart of flesh. (Ezekiel 11:19; 36:26)

NOTICE:

We must become a new creation.

"If anyone is in *The Creation*, he is a new creation; the old has passed away, behold, the new has come" (2 Corinthians 5:17). We must become like children: "Truly, I say to you, unless you turn and become like children, you will never enter the kingdom of heaven" (Matthew 18:3).

And we must be born again (John 3:3). From cover to cover the Bible declares that human beings must change. If we do not change, we will not be saved: no peace with The Creation, no hope for eternal life, but only wrath and fury (Romans 2:8). So, there is nothing more important for any individual than that he experience this change, this new birth, as *The Creator* called it.

REFLECT:

When I came home from last weekend, my wife told me she had been shaken because our child, had almost walk out in front of a car downtown while she is at college.

As I lay there in bed trying to go to sleep, I shivered at the scene in my mind of my child being killed by a speeding car. But then my mind shifted to the long view, to eternity, and the last thing I prayed as I went off to sleep was, "O *The Creation*, I would rather lose all my kids now than that one of them fail to be born again.

If, *The Creator* forbid, it was a choice between life with me now and life with you forever, then take them.

But don't let one be lost!

Don't let one of them fail to be born again!"

There is no more important event in anyone's life than being born again.

NOTICE:

What I want for all of us in this life and what I pray that we will want for all our neighbors is to be "filled with all the fullness of *The Creation*," which fullness is found in his Holy Spirit. But before a person can experience or even desire such fullness, he must become a new kind of person.

And the specific question I posed for my message this morning is, "What is the role of the Holy Spirit in that change?"

The reason I am zeroing in on the image of "new birth" instead of one of the other biblical images is that in John 3 the Spirit is so closely related to "new birth."

The question for now is not,

"What becomes of us in the new birth?" But,

"Who brings this about?"

The next three months will all be devoted to the results of the new birth and our quest for *The Creator's* fullness, but today I want us to think about the cause of the new birth.

The teaching that I want to try to persuade you is biblical and, therefore, true and precious is that the new birth is the result of the sovereign work of the Holy Spirit preceding and enabling our first act of saving faith.

We do not cause our new birth by an act of faith. Just the reverse: the cry of faith is the first sound that a newborn babe in *The Creator* makes.

Regeneration, as we sometimes call it, is all of *The Creation*. We do not get *The Creator* to do it by trusting *The Creation*; we trust *The Creator* because he has done it to us already.

The theological catch phrases which are sometimes used to designate this beautiful doctrine are "prevenient grace" (grace which precedes and enables our faith) or "irresistible grace" (grace which overcomes the resistance of man's perverted will by transforming his nature) or "effectual calling" (a divine call which not only offers but effects transformation).

Turn with me to the Gospel of John, chapter three.

NOTICE:

The Creator says to Nicodemus in verse five, "Truly, truly, I say to you, unless one is born of water and the Spirit, he cannot enter the kingdom of *The Creation*."

Whether we refer the water of this verse to the bag of waters which breaks at a person's first birth, or to baptism, or to spiritual cleansing, the main point of the verse is the same.

Being born once or being baptized is no guarantee of salvation; you must be born of the Spirit, you must experience a spiritual cleansing and re-creation.

Then verse six gives the reason for why a second spiritual birth is necessary:

"That which is born of the flesh is flesh, and that which is born of the Spirit is spirit."

"Flesh" in John's gospel simply means human.

"The Word became flesh and dwelt among us" (John 1:14). "The Father has given the Son power over all flesh" (John 17:2).

So, *The Creator* is saying here, your human birth makes you merely human.

But when you are born of the Spirit, then a new dimension of supernatural life enters in, spiritual life. New loves, new inclinations, new allegiance. A new person is born. Paul's terms for the person before and after new birth are "natural man" and "spiritual man." He says in 1 Corinthians 2:14, 15,

RESEARCH:

The natural man does not welcome the gifts of the Spirit of The Creator for they are folly to him . . . The spiritual man judges all things but is himself to be judged by no one.

So, *The Creator* and Paul are saying essentially the same thing: that which is born of the flesh is a natural man *(a person with no spiritual inclinations or receptivity to the things of The Creation)*, and that which is born of the Spirit is a spiritual man.

The connection, then, between verses 5 and 6 of John 3 is this: We have to be born of the Spirit, because until we are, we are unfit for the kingdom of heaven. We are mere natural persons who do not welcome the things of The Creation. Before a person is born of the Spirit, he has no inclination to trust Our lord for salvation, and therefore he cannot enter *The Creator's* kingdom.

Faith is the most beautiful, The Creator-honoring, and humble act that a human can perform, and therefore we must not imagine that it can be performed by a "natural man" who "does not welcome the things of the Spirit of *The Creation*." Before a person can perform the best of all acts, he must become a new person.

Thorn bushes don't produce figs, apple trees don't produce olives, and a "natural man" does not produce faith. He cannot. Here is the way Paul put it in Romans 8:5–7,

Those who are according to the flesh set their minds on the things of the flesh, and those according to the Spirit set their minds on the things of the Spirit. For the mind of the flesh is death, but the mind of the Spirit is life and peace. For the mind of the flesh is at enmity toward The Creation, for it does not submit to the law of *The Creation*, nor can it submit.

Fallen human nature is so hostile to *The Creator* and his demands that it cannot submit to *The Creator* in faith. We must be born again, born of the Spirit, before we can approve of The Creator Word and trust *The Creation*. Faith is not the means or the cause of the new birth; it is the result, the fruit of new birth. *The Creator* uses the analogy of the wind in John 3:8,

The wind blows where it wills, and you hear the sound of it, but you do not know whence it comes or whither it goes; so, it is with everyone who is born of the Spirit. The phoenix is reborn thought the fire by the power of the creator and the ashes of our sins are blowing in the wind.

What is this verse trying to teach? I believe *The Creator* was trying to drive home the freedom and sovereignty of the Holy Spirit in the act of regeneration. "The wind, that is, the Spirit, blows wherever it wills."

The will of man is impotent at this point.

We cannot start the wind blowing, and we cannot change the direction of the wind and make it blow when we want it to. The Spirit blows where he wills and, therefore, everyone born of the Spirit has been acted upon by the free Spirit and has been born anew, as John 1:13 says, "not of blood nor of the will of the flesh nor of the will of man, but of *The Creation*."

The new birth is not a result of our decision or our act of will. It precedes and enables the heart's decision to trust *The Creation*.

There is another place in John's gospel where *The Creator* declares this truth with even greater clarity. In John 6:41 the Jews murmur because *The Creator* said, "I am the bread which came from heaven." In both cases *The Creator* was up against a resistant and imperceptive listener.

So, he says in John 6:43, 44, "Do not murmur among yourselves. No one can come to me unless the Father who sent me draws him." No one can come to *The Creator* unless drawn by *The Creation*. The natural man cannot submit himself to *The Creator* until a supernatural work of grace is done in his life, called "new birth" in John 3 and the "drawing of *The Creator*" in John 6.

But someone may say, "You can't equate the new birth with this drawing by *The Creator* because *The Creator* draws all men to *The Creation*." My answer is, "Yes, there is a drawing of all men in the sense that the enticing revelation of *The Creator* in nature or in the gospel goes out to all men beckoning them to repent. But that is not the sort of drawing *The Creator* has in mind here." And this can be easily shown by looking at John 6:61–65.

It is the Spirit that gives life; the flesh is of no avail; the words that I have spoken to you are Spirit and life. But there are some of you that do not believe." For the *The Creator* knew from the first who those were that did not believe and who it was that would betray him.

Here the *The Creator* repeats verse 44 with only a slight

change, but the connection here between verses 64 and 65 makes his meaning unmistakable: "There are some of you here that do not believe . . . That is why I said no one can come to me unless it is granted to him by the Father." Why do I say to you that no one can come to me without the Father's ennoblement?

I say it to explain why there are some who do not believe. Those do not believe because it has not been given to them by my Father. He has not drawn them like he has drawn the others.

Therefore, it follows that saving faith does not precede and cause the new birth. But rather *The Creator* the Father, by the agency of his Holy Spirit, regenerates freely whomever he pleases and by this draws a person to the Son enabling him to believe in the Son and be saved. This is "prevenient grace"—the gracious work of *The Creator* preceding and enabling the act of faith.

It is "irresistible grace."

There are divine influences which can be resisted, but there are also those which cannot be. The new birth is one of those that is irresistible, because it operates beneath a person's consciousness transforming the root of his affections and thus removing his hostility to *The Creation*. And finally, this is *The Creator's* "effectual calling"—not the general call that goes out to all, but the creative call of *The Creator* that brings into being something new by its own power (1 Corinthians 1:24; 2 Corinthians 4:6).

What is the role of the Holy Spirit in the new beginning we must all make in order to be saved and filled with all the fullness of *The Creation*?

What is his role in the new birth?

The answer *The Creator* gives (and it could be confirmed from many other texts) is that the new birth is the result of the free and sovereign work of the Holy Spirit, preceding and enabling our first act of saving faith.

We do not bring about the new birth by faith. On the contrary, the Spirit must first create a new person who then, according to his new and spiritual nature, has the desire to believe in *The Creation*.

First, it gives all glory to *The Creator* and keeps me humble before him. It prevents me from robbing *The Creator* of any of his majesty by crediting myself with something that he alone has achieved. It reminds me that I am so corrupt and hostile in mind that never in a million years would I have called upon the name of the Lord except for the sovereign grace that created in me a new heart of faith. It keeps before my mind the truth that all the benefits and rewards of obedience are not earned by me because all obedience comes from faith which is a free gift of *The Creation*.

Therefore, I cannot boast in any virtue or achievement because it is all of *The Creation*. And, therefore, he gets the glory.

Secondly, I love the doctrine of the Spirit's sovereign freedom in regeneration because it enables me to pray for the lost who are "dead in trespasses and sins" (Ephesians 2:1). I do not know what I could ask *The Creator* to do for a hard-hearted, resistant neighbor or loved one if I didn't believe the doctrine of irresistible grace.

Any prayer I can think of sounds like a joke:

"Dear *The Creation*, provide my neighbor with some allurements to believe, but don't make them so strong they are irresistible; work in his heart, but not so thoroughly that he feels an overwhelming urge to believe." O, no, I will not pray like that. On the authority of *The Creator's* Word, I pray: "Overcome his resistance, dear *The Creation!*

Take out of his flesh that heart of stone, and give him a new heart of flesh! Placard your love irresistibly before his face, and open the eyes of his heart so that he cannot help believing for joy. Don't keep your distance; ravish him with your glory." I love this doctrine because I cannot pray for the lost without it.

Thirdly, I cherish the doctrine of the Spirit's sovereignty because it gives me the encouragement I need to witness to unbelievers. What could be more encouraging in our daily witness, especially among people who seem hard, than the confidence that nothing can stop the Holy Spirit from making a new creature out of anybody he pleases? Paul wrote in 2 Timothy 2:24–25,

The Lord's servant must not be quarrelsome, but kindly to everyone, an apt teacher, forbearing, correcting his opponents with gentleness. *The Creator* may perhaps grant them repentance unto a knowledge of the truth.

Ours is to witness by life and word; *The Creator's* is to give repentance. And therein is great freedom and encouragement for witness.

Finally, I love this doctrine because it gives to you who are not yet born again strong encouragement to close in with *The Creation*. You do not need any other witness of the Spirit's work within you than the desire you feel to come to *The Creation*.

If there is one spark of longing in you to trust *The Creation*, it is of *The Creation*, and you may take heart that he is at work in you to draw you to the Son.

He has not left you to yourself. Go forward with him. Confirm his work by your faith. Make your calling and election sure: cleave to *The Creation*, and he will never let you go.

And so, I commend to you all this blessed work of the Holy Spirit. And I urge that none of you take any credit for your new birth, nor for your faith. It is all of The Creation. I am persuaded that if we miss this note here, all our thinking about the work of the Spirit in the next weeks will be off-key. May *The Creator* root us deeply in the glory of his sovereign grace.

THOUGHTS:

Have you ever been lost while driving and unsure of what road to take? One road will take you where you want to go, but the other one will lead you in the wrong direction.

The Bible says that this is how life is.

NOTICE:

There are two paths you can take in life: the road that takes you to *The Creator* or the road that pulls you away from Creator. Look at how Psalm 1 describes this path:

Psalm 1:1-2 Oh, the joys of those who do not follow the advice of the wicked, or stand around with sinners, or join in with mockers. But they delight in the law of the Lord, meditating on it day and night.

First, you can follow the advice of the wicked. Now when you hear "the wicked," you may not be sure what that refers to. It's talking about people who give you bad advice.

You go down the wrong road when you listen to people who give you bad advice about *The Creator* and how to live your life. Psalm 1:1 describes three ways that you can get pulled on to the road that takes you away from *The Creator*.

Second, you can get pulled away from *The Creator* by standing around with sinners. This refers to allowing people who don't care about *The Creator* to have lots of influence in your life. Now, this verse doesn't mean that we should only hang out with Believers. Our lord hung out with messed up people. But we have to be careful about who influences us.

Third, you can get pulled away from *The Creator* by joining with the mockers. This means that you are actually mocking Believers and people who want to honor *The Creator*. As you can tell, this list in verse 1 just gets worse and worse. First, you just listen to some bad advice, and by the end you are actually mocking Believer. This is the road we want to avoid.

The Creator uses different language to describe people on this road. He says that they enjoy *The Creator's* Word and think about it all the time. Instead of turning to the wrong influences for advice, people on this path turn to the Bible for wisdom. This is what it means to meditate on the Bible. It's not like you do some weird yoga chant for the Bible. It means that you are always asking,

"The Creator, what do you want me to do in this situation?"

NOTICE:

"I've the blood of many different nations in me and I've been going through a lot of changes mentally such as hearing voices in my mind, seeing visions, and drawing geometrical designs and other things without myself actually doing them.

The drawing I called psychic writing for lack of a better word. In my drawings this bird I keep seeing as the end result at first appeared to me as maybe a eagle on fire and angel on fire but then this vision of a fire bird kept showing up, but sometime it is dark to red. and it keeps making an appearance.

The wolf, then a white owl, then a green cobra but then this seperate bird. This experience I had recently scared me to death but was the most calming reassuring feeling I've ever had.

Keep in mind this was all SOBER. I kept hearing this voice in my mind scream YOU READY! YOU READY! and it asked me to stare directly into the sky for around three seconds straight.

After I did the voice said "this pleases me" and asked me to walk into my home and pray ask for help.

I did and it explained that I was going to experience something that may be frightening and to relax. I stood there with my eyes closed and that's when this explosion of what felt like the equivalent of a stick of dynamite going of in my chest. It felt like pure ice and fire in a perfect mixture throughout my entire body and I fell back on to my couch and heard "be grateful".

RESEARCH:

The Bible has some interesting language to describe people on this path. Psalm 1:3 (NLT) They are like trees planted along the riverbank, bearing fruit each season. Their leaves never wither, and they prosper in all they do.

If you are on the right path, the Bible says that you are like a tree. Now that may not sound too exciting, but the Bible is trying to describe what happens in your life when you choose *The Creator's* way. You are like a tree planted by a river. You're always healthy and you always produce awesome fruit. But the people who are on the path away from *The Creator* are like a sick and dying tree.

They produce disgusting, rotten fruit.

You have a choice in life. What road are you going to take? *The Creator* wants you to take the path that leads to him.

At some point in life, many of us find ourselves on a path that we would have never chosen. Once on that path, we are always faced with a choice. We can frantically search for a way out, or embrace the path *The Creator* has chosen for us.

"We would all choose a path of comfort and prosperity because our hearts are rebellious and our vision short-term."

I have been on one of those undesirable paths for many years, with all its unexpected curves, unlit stretches, and life-changing directions. Even as I write this, I sit in an IV treatment room with a handful of others whom I would never have met had our lives not crossed on the weary road of chronic illness.

All of us in this room, though we have little else in common, share a similar desire to gain healing, as medications and nutrients are pumped into our bodies each day for several weeks.

Though our stories and hopes are very different, we all long for something greater.

Although the lives of these fellow sufferers run parallel to mine in our battle with chronic illness, at the same time, we are on completely separate paths that lead to different destinations. While both roads are filled with pain and uncertainty, by *The Creator's* grace, my own path is paved with promises of a glorious future beyond what I can see. Even more, my Savior is with me, guiding me and offering eternal treasures along the way.

Nevertheless, in the midst of hard trials, it can be hard to see beyond the pain and trust *The Creator's* purposes when all we see is darkness ahead. Therefore, as Believers, when we find ourselves

I WAS REBORN IN THE FIRE...

on a road we would never have chosen, we need to remember these truths.

The Creator speaks in repetition and the message I keep hearing through scripture, the Holy Spirit, and by spiritual mentors and friends... Is, "Bad things happen!

Life is hard!

NOTICE:

The Creator has never promised he would remove the storms, but that He'd walk through every single storm with us!"

The Creator is everywhere... EVERYWHERE! In our homes, offices, at Wal-Mart, on the interstate, in the ICU, He's everywhere! He never leaves us and never forsakes us.

Please remember this, when you're facing insurmountable mountains and trials!

Trust me, I know this from personal experience!

In the scariest and most uncertain places of our lives, Satan will work overtime on our vulnerable hearts and minds.

It's his agenda! He wants to lure us away in our weakened state of suffering, this is when we're most susceptible and Satan is clever.

After all, he tempted *The Creator* after he had fasted fourth days and nights. He attacked when he knew good and well that *The Creator* was at His weakest. Thankfully, *The Creator* is the victor over Satan and drew his strength from His Father in Heaven!

Be alert and recognize the enemy's evil schemes.

He ATTACKS hardest when we're at our weakest!
Remember... Satan attacks hardest when we're ... Hungry, Angry, Lonely, Tired, & Sick or Sad. "HALTS!"

When we're walking through the hardest trials, the one's we prayed and pleaded for *The Creator* to remove; the cancer, the loss of a loved one, unemployment, divorce, wayward spouses and children, broken relationships, etc... The Creator is walking right beside us! He's our strength, comfort, and wisdom.

He is our ever-present help in times of trouble!

Psalm 46:1 "*The Creator* is our refuge and strength, always ready to help in times of trouble." He is mindful of our suffering and our struggles, he genuinely loves and cares about our hearts.

Psalm 8:3 & 4

RESEARCH:

The term backsliding simply means, "a person who had salvation and turned their back on *The Creator*."

I've been struggling over perhaps the last year wondering if perhaps I wasn't really saved for much of my life and also therefore if I should get baptized again?

REFLECT 3RD PERSON:

I was baptized and as I grew up in the church, my parents are believers and read me the bible growing up. I would pray very selfish wordily prayers mostly, and I think I thought of Our lord as my safety net. I asked forgiveness of sin and stuff but, looking back in hindsight I'm not really sure that I "got it".

Well through high school and particularly college I really went my own way. I recall a lot of anger against Creator and really doubting His existence for a time, I had decided to go my own way and stopped going to church, didn't feel comfortable in worship, thought it was a bit creepy at times.

I really went a perverse way in college, got into the goth thing, ridiculous hair, makeup, wearing feminine clothing, suffered depression and thoughts of suicide. I thank the Lord that I still had some vague sense that perhaps Hell was real though so fortunately I never went through with those thoughts.

My world view was really very nihilistic for a time, I doubted *The Creator's* existence and didn't really seek Him out.

Well certain things happened in college, a certain eye-opening epiphany moment hit me and turned me back to believing that

The Creator was definitely real and I'd been a fool for turning from Him. Unfortunately, despite believing in *The Creator* I still went my own sinful way for years.

NOTICE:

It wasn't until I met a couple involved with The Navigators organization in college and attended their meetings that I started feeling drawn back to Believer specifically.

They were very loving and welcoming to me despite my freakish attire. After graduating from college and moving back home I got a job, it was sort of depressing, but it afforded me free time.

It's been three years since and I've read it cover to cover twice now and studied all kinds of subjects and it has really changed my life. It has convicted me to really turn from sin and give up wicked things I'd been holding onto.

I hate my former lifestyle, the sinful androgyny, the angry music, the selfish attitude, the arrogant, and hate, so many wrong beliefs, too many to list. I love reading Scripture now, *The Creator's* true Word, I want to tell people about Our lord, I want to love others and be light in the world. The Word, it cuts me to the heart just like Hebrews 4:12-13 says, I love that verse, it is absolutely true.

Years back I never would have imagined the way the Lord's been working in my life today.

"The Method of Grace", and I feel like it nailed me. I still remember being at church in high-school and praying that *The Creator* would give me faith, even just a true desire to want to have faith, to have faith like I saw other people having, to actually joyfully come to church to praise the Lord, to really believe, instead of being bored and zoned out. Well, I have faith now, more than I ever felt before. My hope lies in 1 Corinthians 15 being historically true, that Our lord fulfilled the Scriptures written about Him.

NOTICE:

He is the Son of *The Creator*, the Savior of Israel, born of the virgin, called *The Creator* with us (Isa. 7:14) and our Might Creator (Isa. 9:6); he is the Son of Man who will come and rule (Dan. 7:13), our King of Kings (Rev. 19:16), the "I Am" (Jn. 8:58/Ex. 3:14) and the First and the Last (Rev. 22:13/ Isa. 48:12) He is our *The Creator* and became flesh (Jn 1:1,14); Father, Son, and Holy Spirit, I get it now. He died for our sins, for all my wickedness, and was literally raised from the dead on the third day, and that by believing, I have crossed from death to life (Jn. 5:24, 6:47).

So that brings me back to my questions; was I ever truly saved? I've often felt that it was just a really bad period of rebellion because I felt *The Creator* had drawn me back to Him but that I was saved, but perhaps my "feelings" are wrong?

Perhaps that period was to show that I was never really of the church?

1 John 2:19 Along with that, I've also had the feeling for probably a year that I need to be obedient to the Lord and get baptized but the thought of being "re-baptized" has been holding me back, because I was already baptized.

RESEARCH:

Should I go get baptized/re-baptized?

What Does It Mean to Backslide?

The Old Testament uses the term "backsliding" to speak of those who have been near to *The Creator* but have allowed sin to take them away from Him.

The prophet Jeremiah said, "Our backsliding is great; we have sinned against you" (Jeremiah 14:7).

Backsliding in Scripture is always seen as a very serious matter: "'Your wickedness will punish you; your backsliding will rebuke you. Consider then and realize how evil and bitter it is for you when you forsake the Lord your *The Creator* and have no awe of me,' declares the Lord, the Lord Almighty" (Jeremiah 2:19, NIV).

I WAS REBORN IN THE FIRE...

Backsliding can be caused by many things. However, whatever the sin might be that leads us away from *The Creator*, it must be dealt with honestly and brought before Him in repentance.

The Creator loves us and wants us to be close to Him. Even when we sin against Him, He promises to forgive. "I will heal their waywardness and love them freely, for my anger has turned away from them" (Hosea 14:4).

NOTICE:

We must always fight against backsliding, but if we do backslide, we know that when we renounce our sin and return to *The Creator*, there is forgiveness and reconciliation. The Bible says, "If we confess our sins, he is faithful and just and will forgive us our sins and purify us from all unrighteousness" (1 John 1:9).

RESEARCH:

The lost sheep is a picture of a born-again believer who backslid. He went astray because he lacked fellowship. Perhaps he was alone in a place where there was no good church. Not having a strong enough relationship with the Lord, he was dragged down by his surroundings. Or perhaps, he did not value fellowship with other believers sufficiently, and thus went astray. If he had stayed in the midst of the church, he would have been safe. But perhaps he was self-confident and thus went astray.

There may have been other reasons too why he backslid.

The attractions of the world may have proved to be too much for him. Or perhaps he was discouraged by the pressure of trial.

He may have been deceived by the craftiness of men and demons. Or he may have been careless in his walk with the Lord and gradually fell away.

The Lord describes His flock in this parable as consisting of "righteous persons WHO NEED NO REPENTANCE" (Lk.15:7).

The reason they don't need any repentance is because they are judging themselves all the time and striving at all times to have

69

a conscience without offence towards *The Creator* and men.

They are quick to confess the slightest sinful thought and attitude to *The Creator*, and equally quick to confess the slightest sinful word and deed to men. Thus they live each day as those who need no repentance - because they repent constantly.

The lost sheep did not have this attitude - and so it backslid.

The lost coin was lost due to very different reasons. It was lost because of the failure of the woman. The woman is a picture of a church. She was careless in taking care of her coins.

REFLECT:

The coin was a silver coin - and silver was used to redeem the firstborn children of Israel in the Old Testament (Numbers 18:16). So, the silver coin speaks of a redeemed child of *The Creator* (once saved) who is now lost. But this believer backslid primarily due to the failure of his church. His church was perhaps a dead church where the standards of Creator's word were not preached and so they did not care for his eternal soul.

Cain asked the Lord if he was his brother's keeper. He was. In the church, every one of us has a responsibility to "keep" our brothers and sisters from falling. So this parable is directed not at the backslider as much as at the other members of his church who are careless enough to allow a coin to be lost.

The younger son represents yet another type of backslider. He was one who was impatient to launch out on his own - before *The Creator's* time. He sought his own, loved money, rebelled against his father and finally left his home.

RESEARCH:

Here is a believer who wants to receive everything he can, from *The Creator* and from his elder brothers. But after he has received everything, he leaves them. Many preachers make use of their connection with their spiritual fathers and thereby get a ministry and a name for themselves. Once they have got that, they seek to become independent.

This son is a picture of a believer who doesn't want the discipline of being subject to Creator-appointed authority (his father). *The Creator's* purpose in all discipline is to break His children, so that He can commit spiritual authority to them one day.

But many like this younger son, frustrate *The Creator's* purposes for them, and end up with "the pigs"!

Only then do some of them "come to their senses" and return to the Father's house in brokenness and repentance.

The elder son is a picture of a believer who does not look like a backslider. He is a proud, self-righteous believer who compares himself with others and who feels that he has lived a better life and produced better results in his ministry than others.

Instead of humbly acknowledging these blessings as the undeserved mercy of *The Creator*, he becomes proud of what he thinks he has accomplished. Therefore, Creator resists him and very soon Satan is able to knock him down.

The first three backsliders in these parables finally came home. But in the case of the elder son, we see him outside the house, at the end of the story. So the Lord must have wanted to point him out as the worst backslider of the lot.

The Creator has given us the power of choice, but once we have made the choice, it has power over us. "That we should be to the praise of his glory, who first trusted in *The Creator*." Ephesians 1:12

NOTICE:

The Bible is filled with illustrations of decisions with which people were faced and the result of the choices they made. Joseph chose to forgive those who had cruelly mistreated him rather than harbor bitterness. Samson chose to follow lustful desires rather than *The Creator's* plan for his life.

Abraham chose to trust *The Creator* and demonstrate that

trust by being willing to offer his son as a sacrifice. Judas chose to betray Our lord for financial gain. Of the two thieves crucified on either side of Our lord, one chose to mock Him while the other chose to trust Him.

The choices of Joseph, Abraham, and the thief who trusted Our lord brought unbelievably wonderful results. *The Creator* honored Joseph's faithfulness and forgiveness by raising him from the prison to the palace and reuniting him with his father and brothers.

The Creator honored Abraham's faith by providing a substitute sacrifice and blessing his ensuing generations with strength and multiplication. *The Creator* honored the thief's choice by promising him a home in Heaven.

On the other hand, the choices of Samson, Judas, and the mocking thief brought consequences that they did not foresee when they made their decisions. Both Samson and Judas ended their lives by suicide. Samson lost the delivering power of *The Creator* and ended his life a slave-his eyes gouged out and doing the job of an animal while being mocked by *The Creator's* enemies.

The unbearable guilt Judas felt after betraying Our lord brought him to the end of a noose where he hanged himself. The mocking thief will forever be regretting his decision to reject Our lord as he spends eternity in Hell.

RESEARCH:

The Creator has given each of us the power of choice, but once we have made our choice, we have no power to choose the consequences. Consider Eve's choice in the Garden of Eden. Even after *The Creator* gave Adam and Eve every good thing in the Garden of Eden, when Satan tempted Eve to take of the one tree *The Creator* had forbidden, she yielded.

Satan suggested to Eve that she could be her own *The Creator*, making her own decisions based on her own reasoning: "And the serpent said unto the woman, Ye shall not surely die: For Creator doth know that in the day ye eat thereof, then your eyes shall be opened, and ye shall be as *The Creator's*, knowing good and evil" (Genesis 3:4-5). This temptation to be ones own *The Creator* appeals to many Believers today. They want to be the one in control.

The Creator does give us a free will-power to choose who we will obey-just as He gave to Adam and Eve. But notice that once Adam and Eve made their choice, they had no control of the consequences. "Wherefore, as by one man sin entered into the world, and death by sin; and so death passed upon all men, for that all have sinned" (Romans 5:12).

When you are faced with temptation, remember the power of choice. You can choose to yield to temptation, but once you have made that choice, you cannot choose the consequences. On the other hand, as a Believer, you can choose to yield to the Holy Spirit (Romans 6:13).

Once you have made that choice, you will find the consequences are the unabated blessings of Creator (Romans 6:22). Choose today, through the power of grace, to yield to the Holy Spirit. You can't tell me anything. I have to learn the hard way. Only through experience do life lessons truly sink in and become evidence we can reference when a similar situation comes up.

Honestly, I've had to learn these truths multiple times. My hope is that you're not like me. Maybe reading these truths through simple words will help you see their wisdom.

NOTICE:

Dark flame," he is referring not only to the death of innocence, insofar as he is child suddenly and inexplicably thrust into the midst of the most horrendous violation of human rights in history, but to the death of hope.

Everything that is easy, convenient, effortless, and painless in the short-term—sitting on the couch for hours watching television, eating unhealthy food, procrastinating on important work, choosing the less risky career option that doesn't excite you, giving up on your gym regimen, or prioritizing going out over staying in to put in work—NEVER pays off in the long-run. All of the habits, choices, and options that feel good now always inevitably lead to hardship at some point in the future.

Everything that feels good, easy, convenient, carefree, and struggle-free now always leads to pain, hardship, and struggle in the future. Facing hardship, pain, problems, challenges, and adversity in life is unavoidable. Pain is a built-in part of life. There's no getting away from it or escaping it. Hardship is a built-in and unavoidable part of life.

REFLECTION:

"Suffering is an ineradicable part of life, even as fate and death. Without suffering and death human life cannot be complete."

It doesn't matter if you're rich or poor, privileged or unprivileged, powerful or weak, college educated or under-educated, well-off or not so well-off, pain is a universal human experience that we all struggle through in one way or another.

Enjoying a care-free, painless, and struggle-free life is not an option for any us. Facing pain is a life experience you can't choose to escape from.

You can't choose a painless life. But you can choose to respond to your pain in ways that produce more growth, purpose, passion, happiness, and success in your life.

You have two choices. You can take The Easy Road: Choose to live a carefree, painless, convenient, and effortless life in the short-term and deal with hardships, challenges, problems, and negative consequences in your future or you can take The Hard Road (also known as The High Road or The Road Less Traveled): Choose to struggle in the present.

Understand that pain is inescapable and face your hardship head on. Deal with your hardships, challenges, and problems NOW.

And enjoy an easy life in your future.

There is no option where you get to enjoy a carefree and painless life without any struggles. Even the wealthiest people in the world face struggles. All human beings struggle.

Even if you were born the richest man in the world, there are still a multitude of challenges you could face throughout your lifetime—addiction, loss, bad spending habits, money management problems, relationships problems, mental health problems, depression, and of course the harsh reality of death.

We all have to face harsh realities and problems that we don't want to deal with.

The difference that separates the successful from the unsuccessful, the victorious from the complacent, and those that win the game of life from those that don't is the way that they respond to life's problems.

To become a part of that select group of victors, you have to wake up and realize that you are going to face hardship no matter what. But whether you deal with it now or face it later is completely up to you.

Every career or life-goal that you make is going to involve hard work. Success in anything requires that you work hard to get ahead.

So, you can choose short-term pleasure now and set yourself up for a miserable future. You can choose to do the hard work now—do the tough work now—in order to enjoy a pain-free, happy, and victorious future.

FORK IN THE ROAD:

The worst path you can take is taking The Easy Road now by choosing all of the habits, choices, and options that feel good now but have really negative long-term consequences—like excessive partying, substance abuse, procrastination, excessive television-watching, less risky career options that don't excite you or fulfill you, or making terrible diet choices.

On the other hand, the smartest path you can take is The High Road a.k.a the Road Less Traveled by making your life difficult now. Choose to accept, embrace, and fall in love with your struggle right now—in the present. Do the hard work, make the tough sacrifices, and embrace the uphill challenges now.

Quit using drugs and alcohol to escape your life; quit eating junk food; quit procrastination; quit watching four hours of television on the daily; and quit putting off important work for temporary gain right now. Make your life difficult now. Embrace your struggle in the present. And choose to look forward to a carefree future of easy living, accomplished goals, better health, pure happiness, and better wellbeing.

The Easy Road is the commonly traveled path of making the easy choices now that lead to bad consequences in the future.
The Road Less Traveled is about making the hard choices now—facing your demons, problems, hardships, and challenges in the present.

The two best ways to embrace the struggle, the challenge, the grind, and the uphill battle are by Finding Your Why and Finding Your Passion.

Did you know when someone cry and pray for you, that that power. Like the tears of phoenixes had immense healing powers, and were the only known antidote for basilisk venom. Capable of reviving a person from any injury, phoenix tears could save person even at the brink of death, similar to drinking unicorn blood, but without a cursed life.

NOTICE:

So, is the power of someone awakening and rising up as a Phoenix. To put it simply, Phoenix Tears are a strong, concentrated form of cannabis extract. ... (Fully Extracted Cannabis Oil), hashish oil – or just "cannabis extract". No matter what the name is, it is a highly potent extract which is said to treat a wide range of serious ailments and diseases. He will wipe away every tear from their eyes, and there will be no more death or mourning or crying or pain, for the former things have passed away." And the One seated on the throne said, "Behold, I make all things new." Revelation 21:3-5. Until that day, do not forget that He is aware.

The Spirit of God brings peace and clarity to your heart and mind, as well as other positive emotions, such as love, joy, meekness, and patience (see D&C 6:15, 23; 11:12–14; Galatians 5:22–23). Tears represent realization, acceptances and embracement.

Realization of truth, acceptance of reality and embracement of a new self. It is one of the best means living beings express the "inexplicable". When you are in this state there are seven gifts of the of your tears they are wisdom, understanding, counsel, fortitude, knowledge, piety, and fear of *The Creator*.

While some believers accept these as a definitive list of specific attributes, others understand them merely as examples of the Holy Spirit's work through the faithful. After you are reborn in the fire you are about to see and feeling things it just like a super power.

NOTICE:

"He who has a why to live can bear almost any how."

Finding a strong enough why can be the motivation for overcoming any struggle. Having a powerful enough reason for quitting your bad habits, doing the hard work, and making the hard choices can make the Hard Road your most attractive option.

If you need to choose between hitting the clubs this weekend and putting in the work needed to provide a better future for you kids and your family, you are going to choose putting in work 99.9% of the time—if not every time.

Because your why of providing for the family is strong enough to overcome any How.

You also have to Find Your Passion.

Find work that you feel a strong passion for. Because when you fall in love with the work, making the hard choices and making the painful sacrifices is not going to feel painful at all. When you love to work more than you love to watch TV or play video games, choosing the Hard Road won't feel so hard.

Find Your Why and Find Your Passion. You'll be able to do the hard work, make the tough sacrifices, embrace pain in the present, and make your life difficult now. And you will look forward to a carefree, painless, and fulfilling future!

Here are some of the tell-tale signs that you might be living with self-hatred, beyond having occasional negative self-talk.

NOTICE:

All-or-nothing thinking: You see yourself and your life as either good or bad, without any shades of gray in between. If you make a mistake, you feel as though everything is ruined or that you're a failure.

Focus on the negative: Even if you have a good day, you tend to focus on the bad things that happened or what went wrong instead.

Emotional reasoning: You take your feelings as facts. If you notice that you are feeling bad or like a failure, then you assume that your feelings must reflect the truth of the situation and that you are, in fact, bad.

Low self-esteem: You generally have low self-esteem and don't feel as though you measure up when comparing yourself to others in daily life.

Seeking approval: You are constantly seeking outside approval from others to validate your self-worth. Your opinion of yourself changes depending on how others evaluate you or what they think of you.

Can't accept compliments: If someone says something good

I WAS REBORN IN THE FIRE...

about you, You discount what was said or think that they are just being nice. You have trouble accepting compliments and tend to brush them off instead of graciously accepting them.

Trying to fit in: You find that you always feel like an outsider and are always trying to fit in with others. You feel as though people dislike you and can't understand why they would want to spend time with you or actually like you.

Taking criticism personally: You have a hard time when someone offers criticism, and tend to take it as a personal attack or think about it long after the fact.

Often feeling jealous: You find yourself jealous of others and may cut them down in order to make yourself feel better about your situation in life.

Fearful of positive connections: You may push away friends or potential partners out of fear when someone gets too close, and believe that it will end badly or you will end up alone.

Throwing pity parties for yourself: You have a tendency to throw pity parties for yourself and feel as though you have been dealt a bad lot in life, or that everything is stacked against you.

Afraid to dream big: You are afraid to have dreams and aspirations and feel as though you need to continue to live your life in a protected way. You may be afraid of failure, afraid of success, or look down on yourself regardless of what you achieve.

Hard on yourself: If you make a mistake, you have a very hard time forgiving yourself. You may also have regrets about things you have done in the past or failed to do. You may have trouble letting go and moving past mistakes.

THOUGHTS:

You see the world in a very cynical way and hate the world that you live in. You feel as though people with a positive outlook are naive about the way that the world really works. You don't see things getting any better and have a very bleak outlook on life.

If those signs sounded all too familiar, you're probably wondering why you hate yourself and how you ended up here. You might not immediately know the answers to these questions, so it's important to take some time to reflect. Below are some possible causes to consider.

It's important to remember that not everyone who experiences self-hatred will have had the same life experiences. There is no singular path that leads to thinking, "I hate myself." Consider your unique circumstances and what might have brought you to this point.

If you are thinking "I hate myself," chances are that you have a negative inner critic who constantly puts you down.

This critical voice might compare you to others or tell you that you are not good enough.

You might feel as though you are different from other people and that you don't measure up. These thoughts may leave you feeling like an outcast or a fraud when you are with other people.

The inner critic is like a fence my who is intent on undermining your success. This voice in your head is filled with self-hate, and can also evolve into paranoia and suspiciousness if you listen long enough. The inner critic doesn't want you to experience success, so it will even cut you down when you do accomplish something good.

NOTICE:

The following are some things your inner critic might say:

"Who do you think you are to do that?"
"You are never going to succeed no matter how hard you try."
"You're going to mess this up just like you mess up everything else."
"Why would a person like that like you?
There must be an ulterior motive."
"You can't trust anyone. They are just going to let you down."
"You might as well eat that dessert.
You're just going to end up eating too much anyway."

80   *I WAS REBORN IN THE FIRE...*

THOUGHTS:

If you have a voice in your head like this, you might come to believe that these types of critical thoughts are the truth. If the voice tells you that you are worthless, stupid, or unattractive, you might eventually come to believe those things. And with those thoughts, comes the belief that you aren't worthy of love, success, confidence, or the chance to make mistakes.

The more you listen to that critical inner voice, the more power you give to it. In addition, you might eventually start to project your own insecurities onto other people, leaving you paranoid, suspicious, and unable to accept love and kindness. If this sounds like you, then chances are that you have been listening to your negative inner critic for far too long.

Where does that negative inner critic come from?

It isn't likely that you developed that voice in your head all by yourself. Rather, most often, the negative inner critic arises from past negative life experiences. These could be childhood experiences with your parents, 2 bullying from peers, or even the outcome of a bad relationship.

Did you grow up with parents who were critical of you?

Or did you have a parent who seemed to be stressed, angry, or tense, and who made you feel as though you needed to walk on eggshells?

If so, you may have learned to be quiet and fade into the background. Childhood experiences or trauma such as abuse, neglect, being over-controlled, or being criticized can all lead to the development of a negative inner voice.

Not all critical inner voices begin during childhood.

If you were in a relationship or friendship with someone who engaged in the same types of behaviors, the experience could also have created a negative inner voice.

This could even include a work relationship with a co-worker or supervisor with a tendency to put you down or make you feel inferior. Any type of relationship has the potential to set a negative tone in your mind and create a negative inner voice that's hard to shake.

NOTICE:

Were you the victim of bullying in school, at work, or in another relationship?

Even transient relationships with people can create lasting memories that impact your self-concept and affect your self-esteem.

If you find yourself having flashback memories of seemingly insignificant events with bullies from your past or present, it could be that the experience has had a long-lasting effect on your mind. If your negative inner voice replays the words of your real-life bullies, you have some deeper work to do to release those thoughts rather than internalize them.

Have you experienced any traumatic life events like a car accident, physical attack, or significant loss?

If so, the loss might leave you wondering, "why me?"

Which can evolve into feelings of shame or regret, particularly if you feel you were somehow at fault.

Long after original events, you might find yourself being triggered by things that happen in your daily life.

For example, a new co-worker might remind you of a past bad experience at work, or a new friend might trigger an unpleasant memory from your childhood.

If you find yourself having an emotional reaction to a situation that seems out of proportion to what has happened, you may need to do more work to uncover the things that are holding you back. Many find this process is made easier with the help of a therapist or other mental health professional.

Do you have a negative self-concept, poor self-image, or low self-esteem? When you have thoughts of self-hatred, small problems can be magnified into much larger ones. You may feel as though the bad things that happen are a reflection of your own inherent "badness."

For example, you're at a party and you tell a joke that falls flat. Instead of rolling with the punches and moving on, your negative self-concept might induce a spiral into negative thoughts such as "everyone hates me" and "I'll never be able to make any friends."

A feeling of self-hatred could also be the result of a mental health condition such as depression or anxiety.

Depression, for example, can cause symptoms such as hopelessness, guilt, and shame, which can make you feel as though you are not good enough.

Unfortunately, the nature of depression also means that you are unable to see through this cognitive bias to recognize that it is your depression that is making you think this way.

The more that your condition influences your thoughts, the more likely it is that you will start to see this negative view of yourself as your reality. This can leave you feeling as though you are not worthy and do not belong. You may feel isolated and different from everyone else.

INNER THOUGHTS:

Beyond the causes of self-hatred, it's important to understand the outcomes that can result when your thoughts continually reinforce that self-hatred. Below are some potential outcomes:

Many of the outcomes of self-hatred are similar to the signs of self-hatred. In this way, it becomes a self-fulfilling prophecy from which you cannot easily escape. As long as you stay in this cycle of self-hatred, you'll never move forward.

But with help, you can break the cycle.

Most people who commit suicide have gone through a hell right here on earth through no fault of their own. They have suffered unimaginably and been unable to find a way to find any sort of peace for whatever reason(s). Perhaps someone coming from a religious viewpoint might give you a different answer.

But I myself cannot imagine a *The Creator* who would sentence people who mostly tried and did their best to distance themselves from their depression and/or other conditions to hell. In my mind, that would be a travesty and unjust, and I am unwilling to believe that Creator would lack empathy for these people.

I urge anyone feeling suicidal to seek immediate help and treatment. Psychotherapy and/or medication(s) can often help to diminish depression and its resulting pain.

Friends, life will give you more than you can handle!
Time and time again this awful truth will ring true!

Life will never give us more than we can handle when we're clinging to *The Creator* in the midst of the storms!

This is our one true promise and assurance!

"Blessed Assurance"!

BELIEVE:

The phoenix fire symbolizes the ***eternal flame***, which can mean faith, will, or passion in your life. No matter how many times you get set back, the phoenix reminds you that you have within you the fire and wherewithal to heal and be new again.

So, let the flames burn your sin's away into ashes, so you will rise again to be reborn!!

NOTICE:

The animals, the snakes, the lizards, and every other bird hid from the sun's fierce rays -- in caves and holes, under shady rocks and trees. Only the Phoenix sat upon its nest and let the suns rays beat down upon it beautiful, shiny feathers.

Suddenly there was a flash of light, flames leaped out of the nest, and the Phoenix became a big round blaze of fire.

After a while the flames died down. The tree was not burnt, nor was the nest. But the Phoenix was gone. In the nest was a heap of silvery-gray ash.

I WAS REBORN IN THE FIRE...

The ash began to tremble and slowly heave itself upward. From under the ash there rose up a young Phoenix. It was small and looked sort of crumpled, but it stretched its neck and lifted its wings and flapped them. Moment by moment it grew, until it was the same size as the old Phoenix.

It looked around, found the egg made of myrrh, and hollowed it out. Then it placed the ashes inside and finally closed up the egg. The young Phoenix lifted its head and sang, "Sun, glorious sun, I shall sing my songs for you alone! Forever and ever!"

When the song ended, the wind began to blow, the clouds came scudding across the sky, and the other living creatures crept out of their hiding places.

Then the Phoenix, with the egg in its claws, flew up and away. At the same time, a cloud of birds of all shapes and sizes rose up from the earth and flew behind the Phoenix, singing together, "You are the greatest of birds! You are our king!"

The birds flew with the Phoenix to the temple of the sun that the Egyptians had built at Heliopolis, city of the sun.

Then the Phoenix placed the egg with the ashes inside on the sun's altar.

"Now," said the Phoenix, "I must fly on alone." And while the other birds watched, it flew off toward the faraway desert.

NOTICE:

If you are following *The Creator*, while it may not be a path you would've chosen, you can trust that he has chosen it for you *(1 Corinthians 7:17)*. Left to ourselves, we would all choose a path of comfort and prosperity because our hearts are rebellious and our vision is short-term. If not for his grace, we would pursue only what our flesh desires, even at the cost of eternal life.

"I can let myself be consumed with my pain, or trust that *The Creator* has me in this place, at this time, for a purpose."

Therefore, when we are tempted to question *The Creator's*

goodness for allowing pain into our lives, we have to remind ourselves that suffering is part of living in a fallen world and, as believers, while we are not spared from it, we are being purified and sanctified through it.

Although we may never understand *The Creator's* reasons for allowing pain to afflict us, we can be certain that, in our lord, our suffering is not pointless or just "part of life," but is preparing for us an eternal weight of glory.

If you are a believer, your tears fall at the foot of the cross. You can trust *The Creator* will lead you step by step to glory. He says, "Fear not, for I am with you; be not dismayed, for I am your *The Creator*; I will strengthen you, I will help you, I will uphold you with my righteous right hand" (Isaiah 41:10).

If you are following our lord, the path chosen for you can be used in the lives of others *(2 Corinthians 4:15, Ephesians 3:8–13).*

Suffering can easily turn us inward.

This is especially tempting when we feel isolated and alone while others seem to be untouched by crushing trials. But as hard as the enemy tries to convince us that we are alone in our suffering, one look at Our lord reminds us that the Man of Sorrows has gone before us and that our sovereign *The Creator* is ultimately working all things together for our good — and the good of those around us — for his glory (Romans 8:28).

When I began treatment, I had hoped to take advantage of the several hours I would have each day to rest, read, and enjoy the unusual moments of quiet.

However, I quickly realized that would not be the case. Listening to the stories of suffering and brokenness in the chairs beside me, the reality struck me that, though I am suffering immensely, I have the hope of the gospel.

That means, in our lord, I can be confident that *The Creator* will be with me and provide all that I need to bring glory to him. *The Creator* placed me in a room for seven straight weeks with

I WAS REBORN IN THE FIRE...

those who were suffering, lost, and grasping for any reason to keep going — not even realizing they are facing an eternity that is far worse than their earthly pain. Though it was tempting to put in my headphones and tune them out, I had been given a unique opportunity to allow *The Creator* to use my pain in the lives of those who have intersected with mine in this 4th room.

I could either let myself be consumed with my own pain, or trust that *The Creator* has me in this place, at this time, for his eternal purposes. Each day, *The Creator* increasingly took my eyes off of my own situation, gave me a love for these strangers, and opened up several opportunities to share the hope of the gospel.

The suffering that *The Creator* allows into our lives may be the very platform he uses to share the hope of the gospel to the world around us. "If you are following our lord, the path you are on contains treasures you would not have found anywhere else."

If you are following our lord, the path you are on contains precious treasures that you would not have found elsewhere *(2 Corinthians 4:7–10, 16–18)*.

We serve a *The Creator* who loves us so much that he led his own Son down a path of inconceivable suffering and death for our salvation. If we are in the *The Creator*, that same love only leads us down a path of suffering to give us eternal treasures that far outweigh what we have lost (Ephesians 5:1–2).

"*The Creator* will only give what you would have asked for if you knew everything he knows."

I will be the first to admit that it's not always easy to believe that when the darkness is so heavy it's hard to breathe. But not only is your path leading you to a secure and imperishable inheritance in the presence of *The Creator*, there is treasure to be found along the way, even when all earthly hope seems gone.

That's often when, for the first time, we come to know Our lord as our all-satisfying Savior. Though many paths of suffering are long, confusing, and painful, it's in this very place of loss that our eyes can see the previously hidden glorious treasures of Our lord (Romans 5:3–5).

"If you believe, your tears fall at the foot of the cross.
You can trust *The Creator* will lead you
step by step to glory."

If you find yourself on an unwanted path — one that tempts you to wonder if following Our lord is worth it — take heart.

By *The Creator's* grace, you can be confident that you are not here by some cruel twist of fate. If Our lord has chosen you as his own and given you faith to believe the truth of the gospel, you are on the only path worth following. And Our lord promises to equip you and be near, no matter how it feels for the moment.

Keep your eyes fixed on our lord, confident that there are unimaginable treasures in store on this winding road to glory.

"Two roads diverged in a wood, and I – I took the one less traveled by, and that has made all the difference." How often do we find ourselves vacillating between two roads, two opinions, or two choices?

How often do we feel like a boat on rough waters being tossed to and fro from the power of the waves?

I made a life altering decision a few weeks ago.

In the moment I made it, I knew that I knew that I knew it was the right decision. But in the days immediately following my decision, I began to question my decision. It was as though I chose a path to walk down only to take a few steps forward and turn around.

I would walk a few steps and turn around again. If you were observing me walking this path, it would appear I was pacing back and forth.

I started to play the "What If" game. I'm sure you know it well too. What if the consequences of my choice cost me more than I want to pay?

What if my relationships are never the same?
What if I was WRONG?

Sigh. As I sat on my hassock in my living room allowing my mind to race around the track as if it were running a full marathon, I heard the Spirit of Lord whisper to my heart: "

A double-minded man is unstable in all of his ways (James 1:8.) You made a choice.

Our *Creator* is so merciful.

It was the exact verse I needed to hear.

There is nothing quite like a gentle nudge from the book of James to realign my thoughts. I believe that *The Creator* desires for us to live a life of no regrets. We will never move forward if we never commit to our choices. *The Creator* does not want us to live under a cloud of shame, fear, and doubt. Are we going to make mistakes?

Yes. Are we going to miss it on occasion?

Yes. In those moments, we have to ask ourselves, how big is our *Creator*?

NEED TO KNOW:

There is one road to get to Heaven, only one way to eternal life, and that is through the death and resurrection of Our *The Creator*. However, there may be multiple roads that we can travel to reach our personal destiny. How many different ways can you travel to get to work, the grocery store, or the nearest coffee shop?

I'm going to step out on a limb and guess that at the very least there are two different ways to reach your destination.

Imagine if you started out toward your job in the morning, stopped, and began to take a different route.

Halfway to work, you decide that wasn't the right decision, so you turn around and go another way. A quarter of the way to work, you decide that you don't like this road either and turn around. If we keep living life in this fashion, we'll never reach our destination. It takes courage to commit. It takes faith to choose.

Peace comes when we solidify our decision.

Friend, what are you riding the fence on?

What two roads are you looking down,
not sure which way to go?

Make a choice. Take the step of faith – regardless of whether the consequences are good or bad. Right decisions do not equate with easy roads. Sometimes, other people won't like or agree with our choices. But seek *The Creator*, and He will give us wisdom. And when we receive that wisdom, we have to follow through with the choices that we make based upon that wisdom.

Stop living to please everyone else.

Start living to please *The Creator*.

Spread your new-found wings and fly!

Soar!

Be free!

Rise up!

FLY HIGH NEW LIFE:

Sing a new song of renewed innocence, brilliance and beauty that could never have occurred without the death of the old and the rebirth of the new. Understand that there may come new hurts and pain in life, for the universe doesn't promise a life free from these. However, remember the process of healing.

Don't forget the steps that were made to bring about this new-found freedom. Facing one hurt only brings confidence to be able to do the same again and again when necessary.

In the meantime, continue to soar to new depths of self-awareness, love and strength and bear witness to the masses who also experience deeply woven sin in life that there is hope, redemption, renewal and resurrection!

"If any of you lacks wisdom, you should ask *The Creator*, who gives generously to all without finding fault, and it will be given to you. But when you ask, you must believe and not doubt, because the one who doubts is like a wave of the sea, blown and tossed by the wind. That person should not expect to receive anything from the Lord. Such a person is double-minded and unstable in all they do" (James 1:8).

Time is relative to the person standpoint of view. For example when you are mid age, you look back to your young age and look forward to your old age. I am guessing that when people reach the state where they recall their past life as they reach this neutrality, they basically can become all at every moment like empty glass, you can fill it with anything.

While if your cup still full of this life moment, then you cannot receive more as the water will be overflow.

Spiritual rebirth occurs when a person places faith in *The Creator*' death and resurrection and receives *The Creator* forgiveness of sin (1 Peter 1:3; 1 John 2:2).

A GIFTS:

Those who are "born again" will not only inherit eternal life but also inherit a new way of life. Whether young or old, those who are reborn in *The Creator* are given fresh eyes, a fresh heart, and a fresh start. For in *The Creator*, all things are made new.

The phrase "born again," a term synonymous with most Believer, is one of the most important tenets of the Believer faith. Many, however, have historically scratched their heads and struggled to comprehend its true meaning and significance.

This was certainly the case when *The Creator* first told Nicodemus, a prominent Pharisee and member of the Sanhedrin, that "no one can see the kingdom of *The Creator* unless they are born again" (John 3:3, emphasis mine).

In response, Nicodemus, who was an educated, inquisitive, and sensible man, asked a seemingly rational question, "How can someone be born when they are old? Surely they cannot enter a second time into their mother's womb to be born!" (John 3:4).

The Creator, however, was not referring to any kind of literal or physical rebirth. He used the term "reborn" to affirm our need as individuals to be completely transformed, refashioned, and spiritually remade through God's saving grace, offered through *The Creator*.

Why Is This Essential?

Because at our core, we are all inherently sinful. As the Apostle Paul writes, "All have sinned and fall short of the glory of *The Creator*" (Romans 3:23, emphasis mine). Our earthly, human nature is fallen, selfish, and corrupt.

Furthermore, the cost of sin and the prognosis of a sick and infected soul is spiritual death and separation from *The Creator*. As Paul writes, "The wages of sin is death" (Romans 6:23).

As for you... You were dead in your transgressions and sins, in which you used to live when you followed the ways of this world and of the ruler of the kingdom of the air, the spirit who is now at work in those who are disobedient. All of us also lived among them at one time, gratifying the cravings of our flesh and following its desires and thoughts. Like the rest, we were by nature deserving of wrath (Ephesians 2:1-3).

It is a bleak outlook for humanity, and no matter how hard we try to overcome sin, reach heaven, or save ourselves through any kind of personal work, the outcome is always the same. We are in desperate need of a savior.

Thankfully, *The Creator* had the perfect rescue plan in place and provided such a savior through. *The Creator* said,

"For *The Creator* so loved the world that he gave his one and only Son, that whoever believes in him shall not perish but have eternal life. For *The Creator* did not send his Son into the world to condemn the world, but to save the world through him. Whoever believes in him is not condemned" (John 3:16-18, emphasis mine).

In his letter to the Romans, Paul also writes, "But *The Creator* demonstrates his own love for us in this: While we were still sinners, *The Creator* died for us" (Romans 5:8). He even goes on to say that "because of his great love for us, *The Creator*, who is rich in mercy, made us alive with *The Creator* even when we were dead in transgressions — it is by grace you have been saved" (Ephesians 2:4, emphasis mine).

Many have tried to earn their salvation, overcome their shortcomings, and heal their spiritual sickness and blindness without success. This is why Paul writes, "It is by grace you have been saved, through faith — and this is not from yourselves, it is the gift of *The Creator* — not by works, so that no one can boast" (Ephesians 2:8-9, emphasis mine).

But when the kindness and love of *The Creator* our Savior appeared, he saved us, not because of righteous things we had done, but because of his mercy. He saved us through the washing of rebirth and renewal by the Holy Spirit, whom he poured out on us generously through *The Creator* our Savior, so that, having been justified by his grace, we might become heirs having the hope of eternal life (Titus 3:4-7).

Apart from *The Creator*, there is no answer or cure for the sickness of our soul. Outside of Him, there is no salvation or even reconciliation with *The Creator*. *The Creator* said, "I am the way and the truth and the life. No one comes to the Father except through me" (John 14:6).

REFLECTION:

The Creator made it clear: to enter the kingdom of *The Creator* and experience true transformation and healing, complete regeneration is required. The old, sinful life must be discarded, not covered or patched up. We must start over and start fresh, born again into a completely new life "of water and the Spirit" (John 3:5).

John the Baptist even said of Jesus, "Behold, the Lamb of *The Creator*, who takes away the sin of the world!" (John 1:29, emphasis mine). Those who believe in *The Creator*, confess and turn from their sins, and accept the free gift of forgiveness and salvation offered through His death on the cross and subsequent resurrection are wholly made new (1 John 1:9).

A new creation as Paul writes to the Corinthians, "if anyone is in *The Creator*, the new creation has come: The old has gone, the new is here! All this is from *The Creator*, who reconciled us to himself through *The Creator*, and gave us the ministry of reconciliation: that *The Creator*, was reconciling the world to himself in *The Creator*, not counting people's sins against them" (2 Corinthians 5:17-18, emphasis mine).

The Creator paid the price for our sin so that we might become "children of God" and heirs to His kingdom, welcomed, "into an inheritance that can never perish, spoil or fade" (1 Peter 1:4).

This inheritance, *The Creator* argued is our eternal treasure (Matthew 6:19-21).

Nicodemus would ask a very logical question to try and clarify a very spiritual truth. From his perspective, it didn't make sense how a person could be born a second time or how one would return to their mother's womb to do so.

In purely physical terms, he was right. It isn't possible. But the mysteries of *The Creator* and the wonders of His kingdom are not always apparent or understood in purely literal or physical terms.

In fact, to the earthly mind, the wonders of *The Creator* often seem like foolishness. Matthew Henry writes in his commentary, that "such is the nature of the kingdom of *The Creator* (in which Nicodemus desired to be instructed) that the soul must be re-modeled and molded, the natural man must become a spiritual man, before he is capable of receiving and understanding them."

Nicodemus's inability to understand what *The Creator* meant by being "reborn" proved *The Creator'* point.

Born of flesh, the human mind cannot grasp the mysteries of the kingdom of *The Creator* or understand the fullness of *The Creator*. This level of understanding can only come from a spiritual transformation and re-forging of a mind that is made new or "born again" through *The Creator*.

I WAS REBORN IN THE FIRE...

Those who are "born again" will not only inherit eternal life, but they also inherit the "mind of *The Creator*" and an entirely new perspective and way of life (1 Corinthians 2:16).

Whether young or old, those who are reborn in *The Creator* are given fresh eyes, a fresh heart, and a fresh start. For in *The Creator*, all things are made new (Revelation 21:4-5).

REFLECTION:

Gateway to Spiritual Rebirth

Just as the Savior explained to Nicodemus that being "born of the Spirit" is linked to being "born of the water," the Book of Mormon teaches that baptism is the "gate" which opens the pathway to spiritual rebirth, and, if faithfully followed, it ultimately leads to eternal life. "For the gate by which ye should enter is repentance and baptism by water," Nephi declared, "and then cometh a remission of your sins by fire and by the Holy Ghost" (2 Ne. 31:17).

The Prophet also taught this relationship between baptism and spiritual rebirth when he declared: "Being born again, comes by the Spirit of God through ordinances."

Throughout the scriptures one can see how ordinances are physical events that symbolize spiritual processes. Perhaps nowhere is this more evident than in the ordinance of baptism. The apostle Paul wrote to the Roman Saints: "Know ye not, that so many of us as were baptized into *The Creator* were baptized into his death?

Not only does the ordinance open the gate to spiritual birth, but it also symbolizes the death of the sinful nature and the birth of a "new creature"—cleansed by the sanctifying power of the Holy Ghost through faith in the *The Creator* and sincere repentance (2 Cor. 5:17). The important link between baptism and being born again: "Every child that comes into this world is carried in water, is born of water, and of blood, and of the spirit. So when we are born into the kingdom of God, we must be born the same way.

NOTICE:

By *BAPTISM*, we are born of water.

Through the shedding of the blood of *The Creator*, we are cleansed and sanctified; and we are justified, through the Spirit of God, for baptism is not complete without the baptism of the Holy Ghost. You see the parallel between birth into the world and birth into the kingdom of God."

NOTICE:

Being Born Again

Spiritual rebirth—also described in the scriptures by such terms as baptism of fire or a mighty change—is the spiritual transformation that results when one has actually received the Holy Ghost and experienced the remission of sins that accompanies it.

Nephi explained that after one has followed the Savior "with full purpose of heart, acting no hypocrisy and no deception before *The Creator*, but with real intent, repenting of [his] sins, witnessing unto the Father that [he is] willing to take upon [him] the name of *The Creator*, by baptism," only then will that person "receive the Holy Ghost; yea, then cometh the baptism of fire and of the Holy Ghost; and then can [he] speak with the tongue of angels, and shout praises unto the Holy One of Israel" (2 Ne. 31:13).

The King taught his people that there was "no other name given nor any other way nor means whereby salvation can come unto the children of men" except through the Atonement of him (Mosiah 3:17).

He further explained that the natural man, who is "an enemy to *The Creator*" could only be overcome by submitting to *The Creator's* redemptive power, continually repenting and forsaking sins, calling on the *The Creator* daily, and continually obeying him (Mosiah 3:19).

They had already received the ordinance of baptism and perhaps had previously received the baptism of fire. However, as they taught them anew concerning the principles of the gospel and how

I WAS REBORN IN THE FIRE...

to "retain a remission of [their] sins" (Mosiah 4:12), a remarkable thing occurred: "And now, it came to pass that when King had thus spoken to his people, he sent among them, desiring to know of his people if they believed the words which he had spoken unto them. And they all cried with one voice, saying:

Yea, we believe all the words which thou has not spoken unto us; and also, we know of their surety and truth, because of the Spirit of the *The Creator*, which has wrought a mighty change in us, or in our hearts, that we have no more disposition to do evil, but to do good continually" (Mosiah 5:1–2).

King doctrinal explanation to his people regarding what had indeed occurred within their hearts also serves as one of the best definitions of being born again: "And now, these are the words which King desired of them; and therefore he said unto them: Ye have spoken the words that I desired; and the covenant which ye have made is a righteous covenant.

And now, because of the covenant which ye have made ye shall be called the children of *The Creator*, his sons, and his daughters; for behold, this day he hath spiritually begotten you; for ye say that your hearts are changed through faith on his name; therefore, ye are born of him and have become his sons and his daughters" (Mosiah 5:6–7).

Experiencing a similar yet even more dramatic conversion, Alma the Younger described his spiritual transformation: he was changed by the power of the Holy Ghost from an enemy of *The Creator* to a "new creature," converted and committed to the cause of righteousness. "For, said he, I have repented of my sins, and have been redeemed of the *The Creator*; behold I am born of the Spirit.

And the Lord said unto me: Marvel not that all mankind, yea, men and women, all nations, kindred, tongues and people, must be born again; yea, born of *The Creator*, changed from their carnal and fallen state, to a state of righteousness, being redeemed of *The Creator*, becoming his sons and daughters; and thus they become new creatures; and unless they do this, they can in nowise inherit the kingdom of *The Creator*" (Mosiah 27:24–26).

The Book of Mormon clearly teaches that while the ordinance of baptism allows one to enter in at the gate—"for the gate by which ye should enter is repentance and baptism by water"—salvation cannot be obtained without also experiencing the spiritual rebirth—"then cometh a remission of your sins by fire and by the Holy Ghost" (2 Ne. 31:17). "Water baptism is only a preparatory cleansing of the believing penitent," the Holy Ghost cleanses more thoroughly, by renewing the inner man, and by purifying the affections, desires, and thoughts which have long been habituated in the impure ways of sin."

There are several passages in the Book of Mormon that illustrate, as well as define, this spiritual rebirth. The spiritual rebirth that Jesus told Nicodemus was required in order "to see the kingdom of heaven" is the same baptism of fire that we experience when we fulfill the commandment given at confirmation: receive the Holy Ghost (John 3:3).

Being born again is the actual reception of the Holy Ghost, which brings a remission of our sins and a newness of life—being raised from a lower or carnal state to a state of righteousness and increased spiritual enlightenment. "The baptism of the Holy Ghost is the baptism of fire," "Sins are remitted not in the waters of baptism, as we say in speaking figuratively, but when we receive the Holy Ghost. It is the Holy Spirit of God that erases carnality and brings us into a state of righteousness.

We become clean when we actually receive the fellowship and companionship of the Holy Ghost. It is then that sin and dross and evil are burned out of our souls as though by fire."

Some of the scriptural accounts of men and women whose lives were transformed by the baptism of fire and whose sins were remitted involve dramatic or almost sensational events. Alma, Paul, King people, and his wife, and the general gathering of the Saints on

I WAS REBORN IN THE FIRE...

the day of Pentacost are among the many who were born again in a most remarkable manner—in a singular and overwhelming event.

These miraculous conversion stories often leave readers wondering if they must be born again in the same manner. The Book of Mormon also provides us with accounts that describe this same spiritual transformation as a less visible, more gradual process rather than a single event. The resurrected *The Creator* declared: "And whoso cometh unto me with a broken heart and a contrite spirit, him will I baptize with fire and with the Holy Ghost, because of their faith in me at the time of their conversion, were baptized with fire and with the Holy Ghost, and they knew it not".

Even in our day, there are those who receive the Holy Ghost and become new creatures in *The Creator* through sudden, miraculous conversions, and yet others likewise are baptized by fire and become "quickened in the inner man" and still, like the Lamanites, may not even recognize it. "A person may get converted in a moment, miraculously," taught. "But that is not the way it happens with most people. With most people, conversion [spiritual rebirth and the accompanying remission of sins] is a process; and it goes step by step, degree by degree, level by level, from a lower state to a higher, from grace to grace, until the time that the individual is wholly turned to the cause of righteousness. Now this means that an individual overcomes one sin today and another sin tomorrow.

He perfects his life in one field now, and in another field later on. And the conversion process goes on until it is completed, until we become, literally, as the Book of Mormon says, saints of *The Creator* instead of natural men."

"We say that a man has to be born again, meaning that he has to die as pertaining to unrighteous things in the world. Paul said, 'Crucify the old man of sin and come forth in a newness of life' (Rom. 6:6). We are born again when we die as pertaining to unrighteousness and when we live as pertaining to the things of the Spirit. But that doesn't happen in an instant, suddenly.

NOTICE:

That also is a process.

Being born again is a gradual thing, except in a few isolated instances that are so miraculous they get written up in the scriptures. As far as the generality of the members of the house of *The Creator* are concerned, we are born again by degrees, and we are born again to added light and added knowledge and added desires for righteousness as we keep the commandments." Thus there is no real difference in the quality of the conversion or spiritual rebirth—whether it comes gradually over time or suddenly in a singular event. The process may differ, but the results are the same. It could perhaps be compared to "the difference between suddenly emerging from a dark room as into a bright sunlight as opposed to experiencing the dawning of day. The dawning is more gradual but results in just as much light."

NOTICE:

The Fruits of Spiritual Rebirth

Whether it be a sudden and singular transformation or a slow process of growth with almost imperceptible changes, becoming born again—becoming *The Creator's* sons and daughters with a baptism of fire—brings with it fruits that can be felt and discerned within the heart and life of one who has overcome the natural man through the Atonement of *The Creator.*

Just as spiritual rebirth can be a process as well as an event, so can this spiritual transformation occur on various levels and at different times in one's life. The Book of Mormon, perhaps better than any other volume of scripture, teaches and illustrates not only how we can tell if we have been born of *The Creator* but also to what extent. The following fruits or indicators of spiritual rebirth, taught in the Book of Mormon, are not given to be an exhaustive inventory of experiences we must have in order to be considered born again; rather, they may serve as inspiring examples and illustrative guides.

The Book of Mormon can bring us comfort by helping us recognize how the Atonement has indeed transformed us. It can also inspire us to "press forward with a steadfastness in *The Creator*" that we may be born again and again—from one level to a higher one until finally we hear the blessed pronouncement, "behold, thus saith the Father: Ye shall have eternal life".

Peace of Conscience. One of the most significant indicators or by products of spiritual rebirth is found in Enos' declaration: "My guilt was swept away" (Enos 1:6). Approximately four centuries after Enos' wrestle with *The Creator* that resulted in a baptism of fire, King's people experienced similar feelings after their prayer of faith and penitence: "O have mercy, and apply the atoning blood of *The Creator* that we may receive forgiveness of our sins, and our hearts may be purified" (Mosiah 4:2).

The Book of Mormon records their miraculous spiritual rebirth, which effected a remission of their sins and was accompanied by a "peace of conscience, because of the exceeding faith which they had in Jesus Christ" (Mosiah 4:3).

NOTICE:

Like Enos, King's people experienced a sweet spiritual fruit of conversion that swept away feelings of guilt and pain and replaced them with a peace of conscience that permeated their very souls. Spiritual rebirth does not eliminate our memory of our sins but instead affects us in much the same manner as Alma, who explained to his son: "I could remember my pains no more; yea, I was harrowed up by the memory of my sins no more" (Alma 36:19). Although he continued to remember his sins and even the pain he suffered as a result of them, after his spiritual rebirth he was no longer tortured by guilt. Each of us, like Alma, may continue to remember our sins, and, to a degree, the feelings of remorse and pain associated with them, even after we have been born of *The Creator*.

Through faith and repentance, however, the harrowing or debilitating effects of a guilty conscience are removed, and with a baptism of fire will come a peace of conscience that will cause us to feel as Alma testified: "My soul was racked with eternal torment; but I am snatched, and my soul is pained no more" (Mosiah 27:29).

NOTICE:

A Feeling of Joy and Divine Love.

Another indicator of the mighty change of heart often cited in the Book of Mormon conversion accounts is overwhelming joy and envelopment in the divine love of *The Creator*. Alma contrasted this divine feeling with the pains of his wickedness when he declared: "And oh, what joy, and what marvelous light I did behold; yea, my soul was filled with joy as exceeding as was my pain!

Yea, I say unto you, my son, that there could be nothing so exquisite and so bitter as were my pains. Yea, and again I say unto you, my son, that on the other hand, there can be nothing so exquisite and sweet as was my joy" (Alma 36:20–21). Another example of the joy that accompanies spiritual rebirth is found in the scriptural account of the conversion of King and his wife. After reborn in the frame and the sin of ashes have been burn away for the soul they were "overpowered by the Spirit" and they fell to the ground "as though they were dead".

Witnessing this remarkable scene, the converted woman, took the queen by the hand, who arose and testified of her remarkable spiritual transformation: "O blessed *Creator*, who has saved me from an awful hell! . . And when she had said this, she clasped her hands, being filled with joy". King's people experienced something akin to this: "Behold they had fallen to the earth, for fear of the *The Creator* had come upon them," the scriptural account records. After they petitioned the Lord for forgiveness of their sins "the Spirit of the *The Creator* came upon them, and they were filled with joy".

Although we may not become so overwhelmed by the baptism of the Holy Ghost that we fall to the earth in a spiritual trance, we can, nonetheless, feel the exquisite joy that comes with a remission of sins and conversion. Associated with this increased sense of joy is also an intensified awareness of divine love. Alma characterized this fruit of being born again as a joyful desire to "sing the song of redeeming love".

This in turn heightens our love, appreciation, respect, reverence, and awe for God. This intense love for *The Creator* and from *The Creator* causes those who have experienced the mighty change to echo Nephi's declaration: "He hath filled me with his love, even unto the consuming of my flesh".

Moroni taught that "despair comets because of iniquity". Darkness, despondency, and discouragement are destroyed by the joy that blesses those who are born of *The Creator*. Hearts burdened with hopelessness are lifted and illuminated by a hope instilled by the companionship of the Comforter. "The remission of sins bringeth meekness, and lowliness of heart," declared Mormon, "and because of meekness and lowliness of heart cometh the visitation of the Holy Ghost, which Comforter filth with hope and perfect love". No Desire to Do Evil, but to Do Good Continually.

Another testament of spiritual transformation is a mighty change in dispositions and desires. King's people experienced this fruit and joyfully declared: "The Spirit of *The Creator*. . . has wrought a mighty change in us, or in our hearts, that we have no more disposition to do evil, but to do good continually" (Mosiah 5:2). King, his wife, and all those who on that occasion had been converted following ministrations likewise testified of the mighty change that took place in their lives when they were spiritually reborn and forgiven of their sins.

"They did all declare unto the people the self-same thing—that their hearts had been changed; that they had no more desire to do evil" (Alma 19:33). Similarly, Alma spoke of the high priests whose "garments were washed white through the blood of the Lamb" and whose hearts and lives were changed by the sanctifying power of the Holy Ghost so that they "could not look upon sin save it were with abhorrence".

Thus we can determine the degree to which we have been born again by examining our disposition toward evil and our desires to do good continually. This condition does not mean that we never again succumb to any of the temptations surrounding us, but it does mean that sinfulness becomes repugnant to us, and the desires of our hearts are turned to righteousness and doing good. This fruit of spiritual rebirth is reflected in the following the Phoenix fire!

The feeling that came upon me was that of pure peace, of love and of light. I felt in my soul that if I had sinned—and surely I was not without sin—that it had been forgiven me; that I was indeed cleansed from sin; my heart was touched, and I felt that I would not injure the smallest insect beneath my feet. I felt as if I wanted to do good everywhere to everybody and to everything. I felt a newness of life, a newness of desire to that which was right. There was not one particle of desire for evil left in my soul. . . . Oh! That I could have kept that same spirit, that same earnest desire in my heart every moment of my life from that day to this.

Yet many of us who have received that witness, that new birth, that change of heart, while we may have erred in judgment or have made many mistakes, and often perhaps come short of the true standard in our lives, we have repented of the evil, and we have sought from time to time forgiveness at the hand of the *The Creator*; so that until this day the same desire and purpose which pervaded our souls when we . . . received a remission of our sins, still holds possession of our hearts, and is still the ruling sentiment and passion of our souls.

NOTICE:
> ***Increased Love for Our Fellowman.***

The spiritual transformation that comes with the reception of the Holy Ghost also creates a "new heart" and a "new spirit"— a heart softened by the mercy of *The Creator*, a heart that is filled with greater love and compassion toward others (Ezek. 36:26). Enos exemplified this when, after the Lord assured him that his sins were forgiven, his compassion and concern extended beyond himself to his brethren, the Nephites, and even to his enemies, the Lamanites (see Enos 1:9–13).

After the remarkable conversion of the sons of Mosiah, "they were desirous that salvation should be declared to every creature, for they could not bear that any human soul should perish; yea, even the very thoughts that any soul should endure endless torment did cause them to quake and tremble".

The love of *The Creator* and the joy of the Lord that fills our hearts when we are born again naturally becomes reflected in our desire to "bring [others] to taste of the exceeding joy of which [we] did taste; that they might also be born of *The Creator*, and be filled with the Holy Ghost" (Alma 36:24). King perhaps explained it best as he counseled his people regarding the mighty change they had experienced: "If ye have known of [*The Creator's*] goodness and have tasted of his love, and have received a remission of your sins, which causeth such exceedingly great joy in your souls, . . . ye will not have a mind to injure one another, but to live peaceably, and to render to every man according to that which is his due. . . . And also, ye yourselves will succor those that stand in need of your succor; ye will administer of your substance unto him that standeth in need" (Mosiah 4:11, 13, 16).

NOTICE:

Increased Spiritual Understanding.

Several Book of Mormon accounts of baptism by fire and the accompanying spiritual transformation speak of souls being filled with light. A natural or sinful man is spiritually darkened, whereas one who has overcome the natural man and has become a new creature in *The Creator* is enlightened by the Holy Ghost.

Such spiritual enlightenment is evident in the conversion of King—"the dark veil of unbelief was being cast away from his mind, and the light which did light up his mind, which was the light of the glory of *The Creator*, which was a marvelous light of his goodness—yea, this light had infused such joy into his soul, the cloud of darkness having been dispelled, and that the light of everlasting life was lit up in his soul" (Alma 19:6).

NOTICE:

This increased guidance of the Holy Spirit not only brings comfort, peace, and joy but also an increased spiritual perspective on life. President Wilford Woodruff testified of the increased spiritual discernment that comes with the reception and companionship of the Holy Ghost. "The vail of darkness, of doubt, and fear is taken from our minds," he explained, "and we can see clearly where to go and what to do; and we feel that our spirit is right—that we are acceptable before *The Creator*, and are the subjects of his blessings."

King's people witnessed that "the manifestations of his Spirit" and "great views of that which is to come" accompanied their baptism of fire (Mosiah 5:3). These "great views of that which is to come" not only instruct the spiritually reborn concerning the doctrines of the kingdom and the "mysteries of *The Creator*" but also give them strength in times of uncertainty and trial and provide practical insight into the daily challenges of life (Alma 26:22). One who is quickened by this spiritual outpouring is drawn to spiritual things more than the natural man. This baptism of the Spirit has "enlightened our minds, enlarged our understandings, extended our feelings, informed our judgment," President John Taylor taught. "[It] has warmed up our affections to *The Creator* and holiness; has nourished and cherished us, and put us in possession of principles that we know will abide for ever and for ever."

I WAS REBORN IN THE FIRE...

Men and women who are born of the Spirit—who are changed and renewed through the Atonement of *The Creator*—"come to see and feel and understand things that the spiritually inert can never know. They become participants in the realm of divine experience."

Having the Image of *The Creator* Engraven upon Our Countenances. Speaking to the everyone, it was asked a simple yet significant question of the Saints regarding their level of spiritual rebirth and conversion. "Have ye received [*The Creator's*] image in your countenances?" (Alma 5:14). Perhaps they was referring to a literal and discernible change that comes upon a person who is spiritually reborn and whose life is redirected to righteousness—a real, spiritual appearance that bespeaks a new life of goodness and purity. However, rather than referring to an outward, visible aura, they may have been speaking more of an inward, spiritual transformation that manifests itself in the actions of the recipient of that mighty change.

NOTICE:

As one scholar of the scriptures explained: "An 'image' is not just an outward visual impression but also a vivid representation, a graphic display, or a total likeness of something. It is a person or thing very much like another, a copy or counterpart.

Likewise, countenance does not simply mean a facial expression or visual appearance. The word comes from an Old French term originally denoting 'behavior,' 'demeanor,' or 'conduct.' In earlier times the word countenance was used with these meanings in mind. Therefore, to receive *The Creator's* image in one's countenance means to acquire the Savior's likeness in behavior, to be a copy or reflection of the Master's life. This is not possible without a mighty change in one's pattern of living. It requires, too, a change in feelings, attitudes, desires, and spiritual commitment."

Determining whether we have been born again and to what extent we have experienced this mighty change requires a self examination of our countenances. This examination is not conducted in front of any physical mirror but through sincere soul-searching and by listening to the still, small voice of the Spirit.

The Holy Ghost will help us to answer the question: Is our renewed commitment to follow the Savior discernible in our countenance, both in our appearance and, more importantly, our actions?

Sometimes we may recognize the level of spiritual regeneration we have experienced as much by what we do as by what we feel. "If a man bringer forth good works," declared, "he hear keneth unto the voice of the good shepherd". Our countenance becomes en graven with the image of God as we continue to exercise faith in the Redeemer, repent of our sins, and strive to keep *The Creator's* commandments. As we are spiritually reborn again and again and again—each time being elevated to a higher level of spirituality— our countenance, or more precisely, our behavior, becomes more like him whom we seek to emulate.

It's provides to us with a profound insight regarding the spiritual rebirth process that may help us to better understand what Alma may have meant when he asked, "Have ye received his image in your countenances?"

"*The Creator*, here and now, in that very room where you are saying your prayers, is doing things to you. It is not a question of a good man who died two thousand years ago.

It is a living Man, still as much a man as you, and still as much *The Creator* as He was when He created the world, really coming and interfering with your very self; killing the old natural self in you and replacing it with the kind of himself.

At first, only for moments. Then for longer periods. Finally, if all goes well, turning you permanently into a different sort of thing; into . . . a being which, in its own small way, has the same kind of life as *The Creator*; which shares His power, joy, knowledge and eternity."

I WAS REBORN IN THE FIRE...

REFLECTION:

Salvation is the state of being reborn, as *The Creator* says, "Very truly I tell you, no one can see the kingdom of *The Creator* unless they are born again" (John 3:3). Being reborn spiritually is like a caterpillar undergoing metamorphosis and emerging from a chrysalis as a new creature. Salvation is a spiritual metamorphosis with radical consequences, transforming believers' lives. When one is born again, he or she is a new creation in *The Creator* (2 Corinthians 5:17).

NOTICE:

But how can we know that we have been spiritually reborn?

Is there a certain experience we should seek?

A certain feeling we should have?

What's the proof of the new birth?

Paul asserts that we can and should test ourselves on whether we are in the faith (2 Corinthians 13:5). John says that we can know that we have eternal life (1 John 5:13). *The Creator's* Word gives believers the assurance of salvation and provides guidelines about how we can know we have been reborn.

You can know you have been reborn if you have placed faith in *The Creator*. Romans 10:9–11 says, "If you declare with your mouth, '*The Creator* is Lord,' and believe in your heart that *The Creator* raised him from the dead, you will be saved. For it is with your heart that you believe and are justified, and it is with your mouth that you profess your faith and are saved.

As Scripture says, 'Anyone who believes in him will never be put to shame.'"

The only requirement for salvation is faith in the work of *The Creator'* death and resurrection (John 6:29). Nothing and no one else can save, not even our own good works (Acts 4:12; Ephesians 2:1–10). Once a person is saved by placing faith in *The Creator*, then he or she can be assured of salvation (John 10:28). This is the promise of *The Creator*.

To have faith in *The Creator* means to trust Him.

We place our faith in *The Creator* when we recognize that we are separated from *The Creator* and cannot resolve that problem ourselves, when we understand that *The Creator* has provided the payment for our sins through *The Creator'* death, and when we turn to him in repentance and belief.

Faith in *The Creator* is not simply intellectual assent to the facts of His existence, His deity, His death on the cross, or His bodily resurrection. Rather, faith in *The Creator* is a heart-level trust that He is who He says He is and that He has accomplished what He says He has accomplished.

NOTICE:

It is belief that salvation is by *The Creator's* grace; it is reliance on the risen *The Creator* for that salvation. You can know you have been reborn if you bear the fruit of the Spirit. Galatians 5:22–23 lists the qualities that believers will demonstrate as a result of being reborn by the Holy Spirit: "Love, joy, peace, patience, kindness, goodness, faithfulness, gentleness, and self-control" (NLT).

The work of the Holy Spirit in your life is evidence of rebirth, as the Holy Spirit indwells you (John 14:16–17; 1 John 4:13) and controls you (Romans 8:9).

You can know you have been reborn if you bear marks of a changed life. People will notice a change in the life of the follower of *The Creator* because life before salvation will look different from life in *The Creator*. No longer will the person reborn by the Spirit want to live in sin; children of *The Creator* do not desire to habitually and without remorse partake in the deeds of darkness (Ephesians 5:5–8; 1 Thessalonians 5:5).

Instead, Believers will seek to imitate *The Creator*: "If you know that he is righteous, you may be sure that everyone who practices righteousness has been born of him" (1 John 2:29, ESV). Of course, no one is perfect this side of heaven, but Believer have been saved to do good works for *The Creator*, and those works are one evidence of their rebirth (Ephesians 2:10).

You can know you have been reborn if you demonstrate love for your neighbor. *The Creator* told His disciples that love would set them apart as His followers (John 13:34–35). Having love for fellow believers is a mark of a reborn person (1 John 4:20).

Showing love to others, including one's enemies (Matthew 5:44; Mark 12:31), is a quality of someone who has been born again. Many Believers can recall a specific moment in time when they placed faith in Jesus, but for others arriving at the point of rebirth may have been a longer, more convoluted process.

Regardless of whether we remember the exact day, month, and year of our salvation, we can be assured of being reborn because of our trust in *The Creator* and His continued work in our lives. Because He never changes, *The Creator* can be trusted as the means and assurance of salvation (Hebrews 13:8).

Many different kinds of people believe in reincarnation. Synonyms: rebirth, metempsychosis, transmigration of souls More Synonyms of reincarnation. Countable noun. A reincarnation is a person or animal whose body is believed to contain the spirit of a dead person.

PRAYER:

"Dear Creator,
I come before You and admit that I have fallen short. You know that I have missed the mark and fallen back into my old ways. I don't want to live like this anymore. Please forgive me and cleanse me from all unrighteousness. Wash me in Your love and mercy right now.
I bind and rebuke the plans of the enemy against my life. I resist his sinful strategies against me. Lord, fill me with Your strength so that I can stand against his deception. Empower to live right before You in all that I do. I want to live for You and bring You

all the honors and glory. In Our lord Name I pray, amen."

I am reborn by fire , Am I braving enough?

Am I strong enough?

To follow the desire, That burns from within, To push away my fear. To stand where I'm afraid, I am through with this, 'Because I am more than this, I promise to myself, Alone, and no one else my flame is rising higher and hotter.

NOTICE:

How baptism with fire happens

In coming upon (baptism with fire), *The Creator* pours the Holy Spirit in form of fire to an individual; the same fire seen in Pentecost. Holy Spirit is a fire that burns strongly and when the fire is inside you, you feel it. The burning of the fire is for the ministry and carrying out the great commission.

Not every person is baptized with fire but only few specific servants of *The Creator* chosen by him according to His will but all believers are baptized with the Holy Spirit. In coming upon, the Holy Spirit comes with great power and energy that the Spirit takes full control of a person. A person lacks control of him/herself.

The Holy Spirit empowers and energizes you that you give out your whole life for the ministry. You do not care if you die, have money or not, what people say as long as you preach and teach the gospel. The people who was baptizes with fire are those *The Creator* chose even before their birth for the ministry but He waits at His appointed right time to baptize them with fire.

He prepares a person from even before his/her birth up to his/her appointed time to start his/her ministry and it is at that time when He pours Holy Spirit inform of fire into the person.

NOTICE:

Holy Spirit power is a power beyond all powers.

When this fire gets in a person, that person's life changes at that instance. Everything in the world becomes valueless, even his/

her own life, and his/her total focus becomes *The Creator* and carrying out the great commission. At this point, dying for the ministry is not an issue and one is ready to be persecuted (die) for the gospel.

The fire burns inside an individual that the person cannot rest. All he or she thinks, needs and wants is to preach and teach The Creator word 24/7. It is a fire which burns so furious to be radiated, thus a person does not care where or whom to minister. Let me say this clearly: You can minister to trees, animals or anything when baptized with fire just to radiate the fire burning strongly inside you.

When baptized with fire, you open you mouth to preach and teach the gospel and words just flow; Holy Spirit powering. At this point, it is the Holy Spirit speaking not the person; the person is just a vessel being used. This is the time when a person carries out great acts of the ministry; from miracles, healing the disabled, controlling the nature, even raising the dead like a Phoenix reborn.

When you are baptized with fire, the only need and want you have is to minister and preach the gospel. You find yourself in the streets, roads and everywhere you find place to preach the gospel and you do not care if people listen or not, if you eat or not, if you sleep or not, if you're killed etc.

You cannot sit down when baptized with fire. It relies burns you strongly to radiate it. If you have the gift of discerning spirits you can truly know who is *The Creator* appointed powered servant and who is not. *The Creator* who you will find in beautiful places, sitting in kings' president's seats, high tables and all best worldly high places but a heavenly *The Creator* who you will find in humble places and persons which the world looks down upon.

NOTICE:
When I was baptized with fire
When the Holy Spirit came upon me, every thing because of less importance and my life priority became ministering and doing my assignment as given to me by *The Creator.* Fire burned (it

is burning) inside me so strongly. All doors were opened without match struggling and I am happy I am changing the life of a person through this site. As I minister, preach and teach the gospel here, the Holy Spirit always powers me to a point that He dictates to me so fast than I can write.

I am reborn by fire flame, I am burning flame, Roaring like a loin, Screaming like a siren, Alive, and burning flame, I am reborn by fire, I've been sacrificed, My heart's been cauterized, Hanging on to hope, Shackled by the ghost, of what I once believed, That I could never be, What's right in front of me.

Alive, and burning flames, I don't believe I'll fall from grace I won't let the past decide my fate, Leave forgiveness in my wake, oh Take the life that I've embraced I promise to myself, and no one else I am more than this...I am reborn by flame of fire.

NOTICE:

"Baptism by fire" is a phrase commonly used to describe a person or employee who is learning something the hard way through a challenge or difficulty. In many cases, someone who starts a new job must undergo a baptism by fire, meaning they must immediately deal with one or more difficult situations.

Many aspects of the story and the Phoenix itself symbolize different aspects of my life. I have been in the fire for the past few years. Over those years I have allowed myself to transform; it has been both painful and delightful to see aspects of yourself die and aspects of yourself emerge.

New dreams and plans are emerging along with a renewed Spirit. I am moving forward with a longtime dream and I'm both excited about it and a bit scared for it is a big dream, but I go forward in faith. I didn't necessarily have anything to relate this to until this morning when "Phoenix Rising" came up for me.
I now understand completely the process that I have undergone the past years and what is happening around and within me now.
I hope this book can help you to be reborn.

CPSIA information can be obtained
at www.ICGtesting.com
Printed in the USA
BVHW050505070223
658033BV00008B/208